Slow Cooker
MAGIC
In Minutes

Publications International, Ltd.

Favorite Brand Name Recipes at www.fbnr.com

Pictured on the front cover: Oriental Chicken Wings *(page 20)*.

Pictured on the back cover *(clockwise from top left):* Mediterranean Red Potatoes *(page 110)*, Luscious Pecan Bread Pudding *(page 146)* and Chili with Beans and Corn *(page 26)*.

ISBN: 0-7853-9119-3

Library of Congress Control Number: 2002117325

Manufactured in China.

8 7 6 5 4 3 2 1

Microwave Cooking: Microwave ovens vary in wattage. Use the cooking times as guidelines and check for doneness before adding more time.

Preparation/Cooking Times: Preparation times are based on the approximate amount of time required to assemble the recipe before cooking, baking, chilling or serving. These times include preparation steps such as measuring, chopping and mixing. The fact that some preparations and cooking can be done simultaneously is taken into account. Preparation of optional ingredients and serving suggestions is not included.

Contents

p. 24

p. 70

p. 148

Slow Cooker Techniques   4

Super Starters   6

Savory Soups & Chilis   26

Meaty Main Dishes   44

Poultry Pizzazz   82

Home-Style Sides   110

Delicious Desserts   136

Acknowledgments   156

Index   157

Slow Cooker Techniques

Slow cookers were introduced in the 1970's and are finding renewed popularity today. There are two types of slow cookers. The most common models have heat coils circling the crockery insert, allowing heat to surround the food and cook evenly. The LOW (about 200°F) and HIGH (about 300°F) settings regulate cooking temperatures. One hour on HIGH equals 2 to 2½ hours on LOW. Less common slow cooker models have heat coils only on the bottom and have an adjustable thermostat. If you own this type, consult your manufacturer's instructions for advice on converting the recipes in this cookbook.

The Basics

• As with conventional cooking recipes, slow cooker recipe time ranges are provided to account for variables such as the temperature of ingredients before cooking, how full the slow cooker is, and even altitude. Once you become familiar with your slow cooker, you'll have a good idea which end of the range to use.

• Manufacturers recommend that slow cookers should be one-half to three-quarters full for best results.

• Keep a lid on it! The slow cooker can take as long as twenty minutes to regain the heat lost when the cover is removed. If the recipe calls for stirring or checking the dish near the end of the cooking time, replace the lid as quickly as you can.

• Always taste the finished dish before serving to adjust the seasonings to your preference.

• To clean your slow cooker, follow the manufacturer's instructions. To make cleanup even easier, spray with nonstick cooking spray before adding food.

Selecting the Right Meat

A good tip to keep in mind while shopping is that you can, and in fact should, use tougher, inexpensive cuts of meat. Even the toughest cuts come out fork-tender and flavorful. However, top-quality cuts tend to fall apart during long cooking periods and therefore are not the best choice to use in the slow cooker.

Cutting Vegetables

Vegetables often take longer to cook than meats. Cut vegetables into small, thin, uniform pieces and place them near the bottom or side of the slow cooker. Pay careful attention to the recipe instructions and cut vegetables to the proper size so they will cook in the amount of time given.

Food Safety

• If you do any advance preparation, such as trimming meat or cutting vegetables, make sure you then cover and refrigerate the food until you are ready to start cooking. Store uncooked meats and vegetables separately. If you are preparing meat or poultry, remember to wash your cutting board, utensils and hands with soap and hot water before touching other foods.

• Once your dish is cooked, don't keep it in the slow cooker too long. Foods need to be kept cooler than 40°F or hotter than 140°F to avoid growth of harmful bacteria. Remove the food to a clean container, cover and refrigerate as soon as possible. Do not reheat leftovers in the slow cooker. Use a microwave oven, the range-top or the oven for reheating.

Foil Tips

To easily lift a dish or food, such as bread or a meatloaf, out of the slow cooker, make foil handles according to the following instructions.

• Tear off three 18×3-inch strips of heavy-duty foil. Crisscross the strips so they resemble spokes of a wheel.

• Place the dish or food in the center of the strips. Pull the foil strips up and over the food and place it in the slow cooker.

• Leave the strips in while you cook so you can use them to easily lift the food out of the slow cooker once it is done.

Starters

Chili con Queso

1 pound pasteurized
   process cheese spread,
   cut into cubes

1 can (10 ounces) diced
   tomatoes with green
   chiles, undrained

1 cup sliced green onions

2 teaspoons ground
   coriander

2 teaspoons ground cumin

¾ teaspoon hot pepper
   sauce

Green onion strips
   (optional)

Hot pepper slices
   (optional)

SLOW COOKER DIRECTIONS
Combine all ingredients except green onion strips and
hot pepper slices in slow cooker until well blended.
Cover and cook on LOW 2 to 3 hours or until hot.*
Garnish with green onion strips and hot pepper slices, if
desired.   *Makes 3 cups*

*Chili will be very hot; use caution when serving.

Serving Suggestion: Serve Chili con Queso with
tortilla chips. Or, for something different, cut pita bread
into triangles and toast in preheated 400°F oven for
5 minutes or until crisp.

Chili con Queso

Mulled Wine

2 bottles (750 mL each) dry red wine, such as Cabernet Sauvignon
1 cup light corn syrup
1 cup water
1 square (8 inches) double-thickness cheesecloth
Peel of 1 large orange
1 cinnamon stick, broken into halves
8 whole cloves
1 whole nutmeg

SLOW COOKER DIRECTIONS

Combine wine, corn syrup and water in slow cooker. Rinse cheesecloth; squeeze out water. Wrap orange peel, cinnamon stick halves, cloves and nutmeg in cheesecloth. Tie securely with cotton string or strip of cheesecloth. Add to slow cooker. Cover and cook on HIGH 2 to 2½ hours. Remove and discard spice bag; ladle wine into mugs. Garnish as desired.

Makes 12 servings

Curried Snack Mix

3 tablespoons butter
2 tablespoons packed light brown sugar
1½ teaspoons hot curry powder
¼ teaspoon salt
¼ teaspoon ground cumin
2 cups rice squares cereal
1 cup walnut halves
1 cup dried cranberries

SLOW COOKER DIRECTIONS

Melt butter in large skillet. Add brown sugar, curry powder, salt and cumin; mix well. Add cereal, walnuts and cranberries; stir to coat. Spoon mixture into slow cooker. Cover and cook on LOW 3 hours. Remove cover; cook an additional 30 minutes.

Makes 16 servings

Mulled Wine

Festive Bacon & Cheese Dip

2 packages (8 ounces each) cream cheese, softened and cut into cubes

4 cups shredded Colby-Jack cheese

1 cup half-and-half

2 tablespoons prepared mustard

1 tablespoon chopped onion

2 teaspoons Worcestershire sauce

½ teaspoon salt

¼ teaspoon hot pepper sauce

1 pound bacon, cooked and crumbled

SLOW COOKER DIRECTIONS

Place cream cheese, Colby-Jack cheese, half-and-half, mustard, onion, Worcestershire sauce, salt and hot pepper sauce in slow cooker. Cover and cook, stirring occasionally, on LOW 1 hour or until cheese melts. Stir in bacon; adjust seasonings, if desired. Serve with crusty bread or fruit and vegetable dippers.

Makes about 1 quart

Hot Mulled Cider

½ gallon apple cider

½ cup packed light brown sugar

1½ teaspoons balsamic or cider vinegar

1 teaspoon vanilla

1 cinnamon stick

6 whole cloves

½ cup applejack or bourbon (optional)

SLOW COOKER DIRECTIONS

Combine all ingredients in slow cooker. Cover and cook on LOW 5 to 6 hours. Remove and discard cinnamon stick and cloves. Serve hot in mugs.

Makes 16 servings

Festive Bacon & Cheese Dip

Mocha Supreme

2 quarts strong brewed coffee

½ cup instant hot chocolate beverage mix

1 cinnamon stick, broken into halves

1 cup whipping cream

1 tablespoon powdered sugar

SLOW COOKER DIRECTIONS

Place coffee, hot chocolate mix and cinnamon stick halves in slow cooker; stir. Cover and cook on HIGH 2 to 2½ hours or until hot. Remove and discard cinnamon stick halves.

Beat cream in medium bowl with electric mixer on high speed until soft peaks form. Add powdered sugar; beat until stiff peaks form. Ladle hot beverage into mugs; top with whipped cream.   *Makes 8 servings*

Note: You can whip cream faster if you first chill the beaters and bowls in the freezer for 15 minutes.

Red Pepper Relish

2 large red bell peppers, cut into thin strips

1 small Vidalia or other sweet onion, thinly sliced

3 tablespoons cider vinegar

2 tablespoons packed light brown sugar

1 tablespoon vegetable oil

1 tablespoon honey

¼ teaspoon salt

¼ teaspoon dried thyme leaves

¼ teaspoon red pepper flakes

¼ teaspoon black pepper

SLOW COOKER DIRECTIONS

Combine all ingredients in slow cooker; mix well. Cover and cook on LOW 4 hours.   *Makes 4 servings*

Mocha Supreme

Caponata

1 medium eggplant (about 1 pound), peeled and cut into ½-inch pieces

1 can (14½ ounces) diced Italian plum tomatoes, undrained

1 medium onion, chopped

1 red bell pepper, cut into ½-inch pieces

½ cup medium-hot salsa

¼ cup extra-virgin olive oil

2 tablespoons capers, drained

2 tablespoons balsamic vinegar

3 cloves garlic, minced

1 teaspoon dried oregano leaves

¼ teaspoon salt

⅓ cup packed fresh basil, cut into thin strips

Toasted sliced Italian or French bread

SLOW COOKER DIRECTIONS
Mix all ingredients except basil and bread in slow cooker. Cover and cook on LOW 7 to 8 hours or until vegetables are crisp-tender. Stir in basil. Serve at room temperature on toasted bread.   *Makes about 5¼ cups*

Spiced Apple Tea

3 bags cinnamon herbal tea

3 cups boiling water

2 cups unsweetened apple juice

6 whole cloves

1 cinnamon stick

SLOW COOKER DIRECTIONS
Place tea bags in slow cooker. Pour boiling water over tea bags; cover and let stand 10 minutes. Remove and discard tea bags. Add apple juice, cloves and cinnamon stick to slow cooker. Cover and cook on LOW 2 to 3 hours. Remove and discard cloves and cinnamon stick. Serve warm in mugs.   *Makes 4 servings*

Caponata

Mulled Apple Cider

2 quarts bottled apple cider or juice (not unfiltered)

¼ cup packed light brown sugar

1 square (8 inches) double-thickness cheesecloth

8 allspice berries

4 cinnamon sticks, broken into halves

12 whole cloves

1 large orange

Additional cinnamon sticks (optional)

SLOW COOKER DIRECTIONS

Combine apple cider and brown sugar in slow cooker. Rinse cheesecloth; squeeze out water. Wrap allspice berries and cinnamon stick halves in cheesecloth; tie securely with cotton string or strip of cheesecloth. Stick cloves randomly into orange; cut orange into quarters. Place spice bag and orange quarters in cider mixture. Cover and cook on HIGH 2½ to 3 hours. Once cooked, cider may be turned to LOW and kept warm up to 3 additional hours. Remove and discard spice bag and orange before serving; ladle cider into mugs. Garnish with additional cinnamon sticks, if desired.

Makes 10 servings

Magical Tip

To make inserting cloves into the orange a little easier, first pierce the orange skin with the point of a wooden skewer. Remove the skewer and insert a clove.

Mulled Apple Cider

Turkey Meatballs in Cranberry-Barbecue Sauce

1 can (16 ounces) jellied cranberry sauce

½ cup barbecue sauce

1 egg white

1 pound ground turkey

1 green onion with top, sliced

2 teaspoons grated orange peel

1 teaspoon reduced-sodium soy sauce

¼ teaspoon black pepper

⅛ teaspoon ground red pepper (optional)

SLOW COOKER DIRECTIONS

Combine cranberry sauce and barbecue sauce in slow cooker. Cover and cook on HIGH 20 to 30 minutes or until cranberry sauce is melted and mixture is hot, stirring every 10 minutes.

Meanwhile, place egg white in medium bowl; beat lightly. Add turkey, green onion, orange peel, soy sauce, black pepper and ground red pepper, if desired; mix well with hands until well blended. Shape into 24 balls.

Spray large nonstick skillet with nonstick cooking spray. Add meatballs to skillet; cook over medium heat 8 to 10 minutes or until meatballs are no longer pink in center, carefully turning occasionally to brown evenly. Add to heated sauce in slow cooker; stir gently to coat evenly with sauce.

Reduce heat to LOW. Cover and cook 3 hours. When ready to serve, transfer meatballs to serving plate; garnish, if desired. Serve with decorative picks.

Makes 12 servings

Turkey Meatballs in Cranberry-Barbecue Sauce

Triple Delicious Hot Chocolate

⅓ cup sugar

¼ cup unsweetened cocoa powder

¼ teaspoon salt

3 cups milk, divided

¾ teaspoon vanilla

1 cup heavy cream

1 square (1 ounce) bittersweet chocolate

1 square (1 ounce) white chocolate

¾ cup whipped cream

6 teaspoons mini chocolate chips or shaved bittersweet chocolate

SLOW COOKER DIRECTIONS

1. Combine sugar, cocoa, salt and ½ cup milk in medium bowl. Beat until smooth. Pour into slow cooker. Add remaining 2½ cups milk and vanilla. Cover and cook on LOW 2 hours.

2. Add cream. Cover and cook on LOW 10 minutes. Stir in bittersweet and white chocolates until melted.

3. Pour hot chocolate into 6 coffee cups. Top each with 2 tablespoons whipped cream and 1 teaspoon chocolate chips. *Makes 6 servings*

Oriental Chicken Wings

32 pieces chicken wing drums and flats

1 cup chopped red onion

1 cup soy sauce

¾ cup packed light brown sugar

¼ cup dry cooking sherry

2 tablespoons chopped fresh ginger

2 cloves garlic, minced

Chopped fresh chives

SLOW COOKER DIRECTIONS

Preheat broiler. Broil chicken wings about 5 minutes per side. Transfer chicken to slow cooker.

Combine onion, soy sauce, brown sugar, sherry, ginger and garlic in large bowl. Add to slow cooker; stir to combine. Cover and cook on LOW 5 to 6 hours or on HIGH 2 to 3 hours. Sprinkle with chives.

Makes 32 appetizers

Triple Delicious Hot Chocolate

Barbecued Meatballs

2 pounds lean ground beef

1⅓ cups ketchup, divided

3 tablespoons seasoned dry bread crumbs

1 egg, slightly beaten

2 tablespoons dried onion flakes

¾ teaspoon garlic salt

½ teaspoon black pepper

1 cup packed light brown sugar

1 can (6 ounces) tomato paste

¼ cup reduced-sodium soy sauce

¼ cup cider vinegar

1½ teaspoons hot pepper sauce

Diced bell peppers (optional)

SLOW COOKER DIRECTIONS

Preheat oven to 350°F. Combine ground beef, ⅓ cup ketchup, bread crumbs, egg, onion flakes, garlic salt and black pepper in medium bowl. Mix lightly but thoroughly; shape into 1-inch meatballs. Place meatballs in two 15×10-inch jelly-roll pans or shallow roasting pans. Bake 18 minutes or until browned. Transfer meatballs to slow cooker.

Mix remaining 1 cup ketchup, sugar, tomato paste, soy sauce, vinegar and hot pepper sauce in medium bowl. Pour over meatballs. Cover and cook on LOW 4 hours. Serve with cocktail picks. Garnish with diced bell peppers, if desired. *Makes about 4 dozen meatballs*

Barbecued Franks: Arrange 2 (12-ounce) packages or 3 (8-ounce) packages cocktail franks in slow cooker. Combine 1 cup ketchup with sugar, tomato paste, soy sauce, vinegar and hot pepper sauce; pour over franks. Cook according to directions for Barbecued Meatballs.

Barbecued Meatballs

Easiest Three-Cheese Fondue

2 cups (8 ounces) shredded mild or sharp Cheddar cheese

¾ cup reduced-fat (2%) milk

½ cup (2 ounces) crumbled blue cheese

1 package (3 ounces) cream cheese, cut into cubes

¼ cup finely chopped onion

1 tablespoon all-purpose flour

1 tablespoon margarine

2 cloves garlic, minced

4 to 6 drops hot pepper sauce

⅛ teaspoon ground red pepper

Breadsticks and assorted fresh vegetables for dipping

SLOW COOKER DIRECTIONS

Combine all ingredients except breadsticks and vegetables in slow cooker. Cover and cook on LOW 2 to 2½ hours, stirring once or twice, until cheese is melted and smooth. Increase heat to HIGH and cook 1 to 1½ hours or until heated through. Serve with breadsticks and fresh vegetables. Garnish as desired.

Makes 8 (3-tablespoon) servings

Lighten Up: To reduce the total fat, replace the Cheddar cheese and cream cheese with reduced-fat Cheddar and cream cheeses.

Viennese Coffee

3 cups strong freshly brewed hot coffee

3 tablespoons chocolate syrup

1 teaspoon sugar

⅓ cup heavy cream

¼ cup crème de cacao or Irish cream (optional)

Whipped cream

Chocolate shavings for garnish

SLOW COOKER DIRECTIONS

Combine coffee, chocolate syrup and sugar in slow cooker. Cover and cook on LOW 2 to 2½ hours. Stir in heavy cream and crème de cacao, if desired. Cover and cook 30 minutes or until heated through.

Ladle coffee into coffee cups, top with whipped cream and chocolate shavings.

Makes about 4 servings

Easiest Three-Cheese Fondue

Savory
Soups & Chilis

Chili with Beans and Corn

- 1 (16-ounce) can black-eyed peas or cannellini beans, rinsed and drained
- 1 (16-ounce) can kidney or navy beans, rinsed and drained
- 1 (15-ounce) can whole tomatoes, drained and chopped
- 1 onion, chopped
- 1 cup corn
- 1 cup water
- ½ cup chopped green onions
- ½ cup tomato paste
- ¼ cup diced jalapeño peppers*
- 1 tablespoon chili powder
- 1 teaspoon ground cumin
- 1 teaspoon prepared mustard
- ½ teaspoon dried oregano

*Jalapeño peppers can sting and irritate the skin; wear rubber gloves when handling peppers and do not touch eyes. Wash hands after handling.

SLOW COOKER DIRECTIONS
Combine all ingredients in slow cooker. Cover and cook on LOW 8 to 10 hours or on HIGH 4 to 5 hours.

Makes 6 to 8 servings

Magical Tip

All fresh chilies should be rinsed and patted dry with paper towels. To limit the amount of heat in a dish, remove the veins and seeds from the chili. Chili powders, ground red (cayenne) pepper and red pepper flakes are all made from dried chilies. Whether you're working with fresh, dried or ground chilies, it is important to know that the longer you cook chilies, the hotter the dish will be. That's why a long simmered stew with chilies may be quite hot, while a quick stir-fry with chilies has more flavor and less heat.

Chili with Beans and Corn

Butternut Squash-Apple Soup

- 3 packages (12 ounces each) frozen cooked winter squash, thawed and drained *or* about 4½ cups mashed cooked butternut squash
- 2 cans (15 ounces each) chicken broth (3 to 4 cups)
- 1 medium Golden Delicious apple, peeled, cored and chopped
- 2 tablespoons minced onion
- 1 tablespoon packed light brown sugar
- 1 teaspoon minced fresh sage *or* ½ teaspoon ground sage
- ¼ teaspoon ground ginger
- ½ cup heavy cream or half-and-half

SLOW COOKER DIRECTIONS

1. Combine all ingredients except cream in slow cooker. Cover; cook on HIGH about 3 hours or on LOW about 6 hours.

2. Purée soup in blender, food processor or with electric mixer. Stir in cream just before serving.

Makes 6 to 8 servings

Note: For thicker soup, use only 3 cups chicken broth.

Butternut Squash-Apple Soup

3 cans (14 ounces each) vegetable broth

2 cups cubed unpeeled potatoes

2 cups sliced leeks (about 3 medium), white part only)

1 can (14½ ounces) diced tomatoes, undrained

1 medium onion, chopped

1 cup chopped or shredded cabbage

1 cup sliced celery

1 cup sliced peeled carrots

3 cloves garlic, chopped

Pinch dried rosemary

1 can (16 ounces) white beans, drained

Salt and black pepper

SLOW COOKER DIRECTIONS

Combine all ingredients except beans, salt and pepper in slow cooker. Cover and cook on HIGH 8 hours. Stir in beans and season to taste with salt and pepper. Cover and cook about 30 minutes or until beans are heated through. *Makes 10 servings*

Easy Vegetarian Vegetable Bean Soup

Mediterranean Shrimp Soup

2 cans (14½ ounces each) reduced-sodium chicken broth

1 can (14½ ounces) whole tomatoes, undrained and coarsely chopped

1 can (8 ounces) tomato sauce

1 medium onion, chopped

½ medium green bell pepper, chopped

½ cup orange juice

½ cup dry white wine (optional)

1 jar (2½ ounces) sliced mushrooms

¼ cup ripe olives, sliced

2 cloves garlic, minced

1 teaspoon dried basil leaves

2 bay leaves

¼ teaspoon fennel seed, crushed

⅛ teaspoon black pepper

1 pound medium shrimp, peeled

SLOW COOKER DIRECTIONS

Place all ingredients except shrimp in slow cooker. Cover and cook on LOW 4 to 4½ hours or until vegetables are crisp-tender. Stir in shrimp. Cover and cook 15 to 30 minutes or until shrimp are opaque. Remove and discard bay leaves. *Makes 6 servings*

Note: For a heartier soup, add some fish. Cut 1 pound of whitefish or cod into 1-inch pieces. Add the fish to your slow cooker 45 minutes before serving. Cover and cook on LOW.

Mediterranean Shrimp Soup

Roast Tomato-Basil Soup

2 cans (28 ounces each) peeled whole tomatoes, drained, seeded and liquid reserved

2½ tablespoons packed dark brown sugar

1 medium onion, finely chopped

3 cups tomato liquid reserved from canned tomatoes

3 cups chicken broth

3 tablespoons tomato paste

¼ teaspoon ground allspice

1 can (5 ounces) evaporated milk

¼ cup shredded fresh basil leaves (about 10 large)

Salt and black pepper

SLOW COOKER DIRECTIONS

1. To roast tomatoes, preheat oven to 450°F. Line cookie sheet with foil; spray with nonstick cooking spray. Arrange tomatoes on foil in single layer. Sprinkle with brown sugar and top with onion. Bake about 25 to 30 minutes or until tomatoes look dry and light brown. Let tomatoes cool slightly; finely chop.

2. Place tomato mixture, 3 cups reserved liquid, chicken broth, tomato paste and allspice into slow cooker. Mix well.

3. Cover and cook on LOW 8 hours or on HIGH 4 hours.

4. Add evaporated milk and basil; season to taste with salt and pepper. Cook 30 minutes or until hot. Garnish as desired. *Makes 6 servings*

Roast Tomato-Basil Soup

Potato-Crab Chowder

1 package (10 ounces)
　　frozen corn
1 cup frozen hash brown
　　potatoes
¾ cup finely chopped
　　carrots
1 teaspoon dried thyme
　　leaves
¾ teaspoon garlic-pepper
　　seasoning
3 cups fat-free reduced-
　　sodium chicken broth
½ cup water
1 cup evaporated milk
3 tablespoons cornstarch
1 can (6 ounces) crabmeat,
　　drained
½ cup sliced green onions

SLOW COOKER DIRECTIONS

1. Place corn, potatoes and carrots in slow cooker. Sprinkle with thyme and garlic-pepper seasoning.

2. Add broth and water. Cover and cook on LOW 3½ to 4½ hours.

3. Stir together evaporated milk and cornstarch in medium bowl. Stir into slow cooker. Turn temperature to HIGH. Cover and cook 1 hour. Stir in crabmeat and green onions. Garnish as desired.　　*Makes 5 servings*

Hearty Mushroom and Barley Soup

9 cups chicken broth
1 pound fresh mushrooms,
　　sliced
1 large onion, chopped
2 carrots, peeled and
　　chopped
2 stalks celery, chopped
½ cup pearled barley
½ ounce dried porcini
　　mushrooms
3 cloves garlic, minced
1 teaspoon salt
½ teaspoon dried thyme
½ teaspoon black pepper

SLOW COOKER DIRECTIONS

Combine all ingredients in slow cooker. Cover and cook on LOW 4 to 6 hours.　　*Makes 8 to 10 servings*

Potato-Crab Chowder

Vegetarian Chili

1 tablespoon vegetable oil

1 cup finely chopped onion

1 cup chopped red bell pepper

2 tablespoons minced jalapeño pepper*

1 clove garlic, minced

1 can (28 ounces) crushed tomatoes

1 can (14½ ounces) black beans, rinsed and drained

1 can (14 ounces) garbanzo beans, drained

½ cup corn

¼ cup tomato paste

1 teaspoon sugar

1 teaspoon ground cumin

1 teaspoon dried basil leaves

1 teaspoon chili powder

¼ teaspoon black pepper

Sour cream and shredded Cheddar cheese (optional)

*Jalapeño peppers can sting and irritate the skin; wear rubber gloves when handling peppers and do not touch eyes. Wash hands after handling.

SLOW COOKER DIRECTIONS

1. Heat oil in large nonstick skillet over medium-high heat until hot. Add chopped onion, bell pepper, jalapeño pepper and garlic; cook and stir 5 minutes or until vegetables are tender.

2. Spoon vegetables into slow cooker. Add remaining ingredients, except sour cream and cheese, to slow cooker; mix well. Cover and cook on LOW 4 to 5 hours. Garnish with sour cream and cheese, if desired.

Makes 4 servings

Magical Tip

When onions are cut, they release sulfur compounds that bring tears to the eyes. Try one of these suggestions for minimizing tears:
• Freeze the onion for 20 minutes before chopping.
• Chew a piece of bread while peeling and chopping.
• Breathe through your nose, keeping your mouth closed.
• Work as quickly as possible; never touch your eyes.
• Wash your hands, knife and cutting surface thoroughly when finished.

Vegetarian Chili

Three-Bean Turkey Chili

- 1 pound ground turkey
- 1 small onion, chopped
- 1 can (28 ounces) diced tomatoes, undrained
- 1 can (14½ ounces) chick-peas
- 1 can (14½ ounces) kidney beans
- 1 can (14½ ounces) black beans
- 1 can (6 ounces) tomato sauce
- 1 can (4½ ounces) chopped chilies
- 1 to 2 tablespoons chili powder, or to taste

SLOW COOKER DIRECTIONS

1. Cook turkey and onion in medium skillet over medium-high heat, stirring to break up meat until turkey is no longer pink. Drain; place turkey mixture in slow cooker.

2. Add all remaining ingredients and mix well. Cook on HIGH 6 to 8 hours.   *Makes 6 to 8 servings*

Tuscan White Bean Soup

- 6 ounces smoked bacon, diced
- 10 cups chicken broth
- 1 bag (16 ounces) dried great northern beans, rinsed
- 1 can (14½ ounces) diced tomatoes, undrained
- 1 large onion, chopped
- 3 carrots, peeled and chopped
- 4 cloves garlic, minced
- 1 fresh rosemary sprig *or* 1 teaspoon dried rosemary
- 1 teaspoon black pepper

SLOW COOKER DIRECTIONS

Cook bacon in medium skillet over medium-high heat until just cooked; drain and transfer to slow cooker. Add remaining ingredients. Cover and cook on LOW 8 hours or until beans are tender. Remove and discard rosemary sprig before serving.

Makes 8 to 10 servings

Serving Suggestion: Place slices of toasted Italian bread in bottom of individual soup bowls. Drizzle with olive oil. Pour soup over bread and serve.

Three-Bean Turkey Chili

Southwest Bean Chili

1 can (16 ounces) tomato sauce

2 medium green bell peppers, seeded and chopped

1 can (15 ounces) garbanzo beans, rinsed and drained

1 can (15 ounces) red kidney beans, rinsed and drained

1 can (15 ounces) black beans, rinsed and drained

1 can (14½ ounces) Mexican-style stewed tomatoes, undrained

1½ cups frozen corn

1 cup chicken broth

3 tablespoons chili powder

4 cloves garlic, minced

1 tablespoon cocoa powder

1 teaspoon ground cumin

½ teaspoon salt

Hot cooked rice

TOPPINGS

Shredded cheese, sliced ripe olives, avocado and green onion slices (optional)

SLOW COOKER DIRECTIONS

Combine all ingredients except rice and toppings in slow cooker. Cover and cook on LOW 6 to 6 ½ hours or until vegetables are tender.

Spoon rice into bowls; top with chili. Serve with toppings, if desired. *Makes 8 to 10 servings*

Southwest Bean Chili

Meaty Main Dishes

Stew Provençal

2 cans (about 14 ounces each) beef broth, divided

⅓ cup all-purpose flour

1½ pounds pork tenderloin, trimmed and diced

4 red potatoes, unpeeled and cut into cubes

2 cups frozen cut green beans

1 onion, chopped

2 cloves garlic, minced

1 teaspoon salt

1 teaspoon dried thyme leaves

½ teaspoon black pepper

SLOW COOKER DIRECTIONS

Combine ¾ cup beef broth and flour in small bowl. Set aside.

Add remaining broth, pork, potatoes, beans, onion, garlic, salt, thyme and pepper to slow cooker; stir. Cover and cook on LOW 8 to 10 hours or on HIGH 4 to 5 hours. If cooking on LOW, turn to HIGH last 30 minutes. Stir in flour mixture. Cook 30 minutes to thicken.

Makes 8 servings

Stew Provençal

Shredded Pork Wraps

1 cup salsa, divided
2 tablespoons cornstarch
1 bone-in pork sirloin roast
   (2 pounds)
6 (8-inch) flour tortillas
3 cups broccoli slaw mix
⅓ cup shredded reduced-fat
   Cheddar cheese

SLOW COOKER DIRECTIONS

1. Combine ¼ cup salsa and cornstarch in small bowl; stir until smooth. Pour mixture into slow cooker. Top with pork roast. Pour remaining ¾ cup salsa over roast.

2. Cover and cook on LOW 6 to 8 hours or until internal temperature reaches 165°F when tested with meat thermometer inserted in thickest part of roast, not touching bone. Remove roast from slow cooker. Transfer roast to cutting board; cover with foil and let stand 10 to 15 minutes or until cool enough to handle. (Internal temperature will rise 5° to 10°F during stand time.) Trim and discard outer fat from pork. Using 2 forks, pull pork into coarse shreds.

3. Divide shredded meat evenly among tortillas. Spoon about 2 tablespoons salsa mixture on top of meat in each tortilla. Top evenly with broccoli slaw mix and cheese. Fold bottom edge of tortilla over filling; fold in sides. Roll up completely to enclose filling. Serve remaining salsa mixture as dipping sauce.

Makes 6 servings

Shredded Pork Wraps

The Best Beef Stew

½ cup plus 2 tablespoons all-purpose flour, divided

2 teaspoons salt

1 teaspoon black pepper

3 pounds beef stew meat, trimmed and cut into cubes

1 can (16 ounces) diced tomatoes in juice, undrained

3 potatoes, peeled and diced

½ pound smoked sausage, sliced

1 cup chopped leek

1 cup chopped onion

4 ribs celery, sliced

½ cup chicken broth

3 cloves garlic, minced

1 teaspoon dried thyme leaves

3 tablespoons water

SLOW COOKER DIRECTIONS

Combine ½ cup flour, salt and pepper in resealable plastic food storage bag. Add beef; shake bag to coat beef. Place beef in slow cooker. Add remaining ingredients except remaining 2 tablespoons flour and water; stir well. Cover and cook on LOW 8 to 12 hours or on HIGH 4 to 6 hours.

One hour before serving, turn slow cooker to HIGH. Combine remaining 2 tablespoons flour and water in small bowl; stir until mixture becomes paste. Stir mixture into slow cooker; mix well. Cover and cook until thickened.   *Makes 8 servings*

The Best Beef Stew

Pork & Tomato Ragout

2 pounds boneless pork or veal stew meat, cut into 1-inch pieces

¼ cup all-purpose flour

3 tablespoons olive oil

1¼ cups white wine

2 pounds red potatoes, cut into ½-inch pieces

1 can (14½ ounces) diced tomatoes, undrained

1 cup finely chopped onion

1 cup water

½ cup finely chopped celery

2 cloves garlic, minced

½ teaspoon black pepper

1 cinnamon stick

3 tablespoons chopped fresh parsley

SLOW COOKER DIRECTIONS

1. Dredge meat in flour. Heat oil in large skillet. Add meat to skillet and cook until brown on all sides. Place meat in slow cooker.

2. Add wine to skillet and bring to a boil, scraping up browned bits in skillet. Pour into slow cooker.

3. Add all remaining ingredients except parsley. Cover and cook on LOW 6 to 8 hours or until meat and potatoes are tender. Remove and discard cinnamon stick; sprinkle with parsley just before serving.

Makes 6 servings

Campbell's® Asian Tomato Beef

2 cans (10¾ ounces each) CAMPBELL'S® Condensed Tomato Soup

⅓ cup soy sauce

⅓ cup vinegar

1½ teaspoons garlic powder

¼ teaspoon pepper

1 (3- to 3½-pound) boneless beef round steak, ¾ inch thick, cut into strips

6 cups broccoli flowerets

8 cups hot cooked rice

SLOW COOKER DIRECTIONS

1. In slow cooker mix soup, soy sauce, vinegar, garlic powder, pepper and beef. Cover and cook on **low** 7 to 8 hours or until beef is done.

2. Stir. Arrange broccoli over beef. Cover and cook on **high** 15 minutes more or until tender-crisp. Serve over rice. *Makes 8 servings*

Prep Time: 10 minutes
Cook Time: 7 to 8 hours and 15 minutes

Pork & Tomato Ragout

Campbell's® Savory Pot Roast

1 can (10¾ ounces)
   CAMPBELL'S®
   Condensed Cream of
   Mushroom Soup *or*
   98% Fat Free Cream
   of Mushroom Soup

1 pouch CAMPBELL'S® Dry
   Onion Soup and Recipe
   Mix

6 medium potatoes, cut
   into 1-inch pieces
   (about 6 cups)

6 medium carrots, thickly
   sliced (about 3 cups)

1 (3½- to 4-pound)
   boneless chuck pot
   roast, trimmed

SLOW COOKER DIRECTIONS

In slow cooker mix soup, soup mix, potatoes and carrots. Add roast and turn to coat. Cover and cook on *low* 8 to 9 hours or until roast and vegetables are done.

Makes 7 to 8 servings

Prep Time: 10 minutes
Cook Time: 8 to 9 hours

Campbell's® Golden Mushroom Pork & Apples

2 cans (10¾ ounces each)
   CAMPBELL'S®
   Condensed Golden
   Mushroom Soup

½ cup water

1 tablespoon brown sugar

1 tablespoon
   Worcestershire sauce

1 teaspoon dried thyme
   leaves, crushed

4 large Granny Smith
   apples, sliced (about
   4 cups)

2 large onions, sliced
   (about 2 cups)

8 boneless pork chops,
   ¾ inch thick (about
   2 pounds)

SLOW COOKER DIRECTIONS

In slow cooker mix soup, water, brown sugar, Worcestershire and thyme. Add apples, onions and pork. Cover and cook on *low* 8 to 9 hours or until pork is tender.

Makes 8 servings

Prep Time: 10 minutes
Cook Time: 8 to 9 hours

Top to bottom: Campbell's® Savory Pot Roast and
Campbell's® Golden Mushroom Pork & Apples

BBQ Pork Sandwiches

4 pounds boneless pork loin roast, fat trimmed

1 can (14½ ounces) beef broth

⅓ cup *French's®* Worcestershire Sauce

⅓ cup *Frank's® RedHot®* Cayenne Pepper Sauce

SAUCE

½ cup ketchup

¼ ⅛ cup molasses

¼ cup *French's®* Classic Yellow® Mustard

¼ cup *French's®* Worcestershire Sauce

2 tablespoons *Frank's® RedHot®* Cayenne Pepper Sauce

SLOW COOKER DIRECTIONS

1. Place roast on bottom of slow cooker. Combine broth, *⅓ cup each* Worcestershire and *Frank's RedHot* Sauce. Pour over roast. Cover and cook on high-heat setting 5 hours* or until roast is tender.

2. Meanwhile, combine ingredients for sauce in large bowl; set aside.

3. Transfer roast to large cutting board. Discard liquid. Coarsely chop roast. Stir into reserved sauce. Spoon pork mixture on large rolls. Serve with deli potato salad, if desired. *Makes 8 to 10 servings*

*Or cook 10 hours on low-heat setting.

Prep Time: 10 minutes
Cook Time: 5 hours

Tip: Make additional sauce and serve on the side. Great also with barbecued ribs and chops!

Classic Cabbage Rolls

6 cups water

12 large cabbage leaves

1 pound lean ground lamb

½ cup cooked rice

1 teaspoon salt

¼ teaspoon dried oregano leaves

¼ teaspoon ground nutmeg

¼ teaspoon black pepper

1½ cups tomato sauce

SLOW COOKER DIRECTIONS

Bring water to a boil in large saucepan. Turn off heat. Soak cabbage leaves in water 5 minutes; remove, drain and cool.

Combine lamb, rice, salt, oregano, nutmeg and pepper in large bowl. Place 2 tablespoonfuls mixture in center of each cabbage leaf; roll firmly. Place cabbage rolls in slow cooker, seam-side down. Pour tomato sauce over cabbage rolls. Cover and cook on LOW 8 to 10 hours. *Makes 6 servings*

BBQ Pork Sandwich

Beef Stew with Molasses and Raisins

⅓ cup all-purpose flour

2 teaspoons salt, divided

1½ teaspoons black pepper, divided

2 pounds boneless beef chuck roast, cut into 1½-inch cubes

5 tablespoons canola oil, divided

2 medium onions, sliced

1 can (28 ounces) diced tomatoes, drained

1 cup beef broth

3 tablespoons molasses

2 tablespoons cider vinegar

4 cloves garlic, minced

2 teaspoons dried thyme

1 teaspoon celery salt

1 bay leaf

8 ounces baby carrots, cut in half lengthwise

2 parsnips, diced

½ cup golden raisins

Salt and black pepper

SLOW COOKER DIRECTIONS

1. Combine flour, 1½ teaspoons salt and 1 teaspoon pepper in large bowl. Toss meat in flour mixture. Heat 2 tablespoons oil in large skillet over medium-high heat. Add half of beef and brown on all sides. Set aside browned beef and repeat with 2 tablespoons oil and remaining beef.

2. Add remaining 1 tablespoon oil to skillet. Add onions and cook, stirring to loosen any browned bits, about 5 minutes. Add tomatoes, broth, molasses, vinegar, garlic, thyme, celery salt, bay leaf, and remaining ½ teaspoon salt and ½ teaspoon pepper. Bring to a boil. Add browned beef and boil 1 minute.

3. Transfer mixture to slow cooker. Cover and cook on LOW 5 hours or on HIGH 2½ hours. Add carrots, parsnips and raisins. Cook 1 to 2 hours more or until vegetables are tender. Season with salt and pepper.

Makes 6 to 8 servings

Beef Stew with Molasses and Raisins

Classic Beef & Noodles

¼ pound mushrooms
2 pounds beef stew meat, trimmed and cubed
2 tablespoons chopped onion
2 cloves garlic, minced
1 teaspoon salt
1 teaspoon dried oregano
½ teaspoon black pepper
¼ teaspoon dried marjoram
1 bay leaf
1½ cups beef broth
⅓ cup dry sherry
8 ounces sour cream
½ cup all-purpose flour
¼ cup water
4 cups hot cooked noodles

SLOW COOKER DIRECTIONS

Slice mushrooms in half. Combine beef, mushrooms, onion, garlic, salt, oregano, pepper, marjoram and bay leaf in slow cooker. Pour in beef broth and sherry. Cover and cook on LOW 8 to 10 hours or on HIGH 4 to 5 hours. Remove and discard bay leaf.

If cooking on LOW, turn to HIGH. Stir together sour cream, flour and water in small bowl. Stir about 1 cup liquid from slow cooker into sour cream mixture. Stir mixture back into slow cooker. Cover and cook on HIGH 30 minutes or until thickened and bubbly. Serve over noodles. Garnished as desired.

Makes 8 servings

Steak San Marino

¼ cup all-purpose flour
1 teaspoon salt
½ teaspoon black pepper
4 beef round steaks, about 1 inch thick
1 can (8 ounces) tomato sauce
2 carrots, chopped
½ onion, chopped
1 rib celery, chopped
1 teaspoon dried Italian seasoning
½ teaspoon Worcestershire sauce
1 bay leaf
Hot cooked rice

SLOW COOKER DIRECTIONS

Combine flour, salt and pepper in small bowl. Dredge each steak in flour mixture. Place in slow cooker. Combine tomato sauce, carrots, onion, celery, Italian seasoning, Worcestershire sauce and bay leaf in small bowl; pour into slow cooker. Cover and cook on LOW 8 to 10 hours or on HIGH 4 to 5 hours.

Remove and discard bay leaf. Serve steaks and sauce over rice. *Makes 4 servings*

Classic Beef & Noodles

Cheesy Pork and Potatoes

½ pound ground pork, cooked and crumbled

½ cup finely crushed saltine crackers

⅓ cup barbecue sauce

1 egg

3 tablespoons margarine

1 tablespoon vegetable oil

4 potatoes, peeled and thinly sliced

1 onion, thinly sliced

1 cup grated mozzarella cheese

⅔ cup evaporated milk

1 teaspoon salt

¼ teaspoon paprika

⅛ teaspoon black pepper

SLOW COOKER DIRECTIONS

Combine pork, crackers, barbecue sauce and egg in large bowl; shape mixture into 6 patties. Heat margarine and oil in medium skillet. Sauté potatoes and onion until lightly browned. Drain and place in slow cooker.

Combine cheese, milk, salt, paprika and pepper in small bowl. Pour into slow cooker. Layer pork patties on top. Cover and cook on LOW 3 to 5 hours. Garnish with chopped fresh parsley, if desired. *Makes 6 servings*

Vegetable-Stuffed Pork Chops

4 double pork loin chops, well trimmed

Salt and black pepper

1 can (15¼ ounces) kernel corn, drained

1 green bell pepper, chopped

1 cup Italian-style seasoned dry bread crumbs

1 small onion, chopped

½ cup uncooked long-grain converted rice

1 can (8 ounces) tomato sauce

SLOW COOKER DIRECTIONS

Cut pocket in each pork chop, cutting from edge nearest bone. Lightly season pockets with salt and pepper to taste. Mix corn, bell pepper, bread crumbs onion and rice in large bowl. Stuff pork chops with rice mixture. Secure along fat side with wooden toothpicks. Place any remaining rice mixture into slow cooker. Add stuffed pork chops to slow cooker. Moisten top of each pork chop with tomato sauce. Pour any remaining tomato sauce over top. Cover and cook on LOW 8 to 10 hours or until done. Remove pork chops to serving platter. Remove and discard toothpicks. Serve pork chops with rice mixture. *Makes 4 servings*

Cheesy Pork and Potatoes

Corned Beef and Cabbage

1 head cabbage
(1 ½ pounds), cut into
6 wedges

4 ounces baby carrots

1 corned beef (3-pounds)
with seasoning packet*

⅓ cup prepared mustard
(optional)

⅓ cup honey (optional)

*If seasoning packet is not perforated, poke several small holes with tip of paring knife.

SLOW COOKER DIRECTIONS

1. Place cabbage in slow cooker; top with carrots.

2. Place seasoning packet on top of vegetables. Place corned beef fat side up over seasoning packet and vegetables. Add 1 quart water. Cover and cook on LOW 10 hours.

3. Discard seasoning packet. Just before serving, combine mustard and honey in small bowl. Use as dipping sauce, if desired. *Makes 6 servings*

Golden Harvest Stew

1 pound pork cutlets, cut
into 1-inch pieces

2 tablespoons all-purpose
flour, divided

1 tablespoon vegetable oil

2 medium Yukon gold
potatoes, cut into
1-inch cubes

1 large sweet potato,
peeled and cut into
1-inch cubes

1 cup chopped carrots

1 ear corn, broken into
4 pieces *or* ½ cup
corn

½ cup chicken broth

1 jalapeño pepper, seeded
and finely chopped

1 clove garlic, minced

1 teaspoon salt

¼ teaspoon black pepper

¼ teaspoon dried thyme

SLOW COOKER DIRECTIONS

1. Toss pork pieces with 1 tablespoon flour; set aside. Heat oil in large nonstick skillet over medium-high heat until hot. Brown pork 2 to 3 minutes per side; transfer to 5-quart slow cooker.

2. Add remaining ingredients to slow cooker. Cover and cook on LOW 5 to 6 hours.

3. Combine remaining 1 tablespoon flour and ¼ cup broth from stew in small bowl; stir until smooth. Pour flour mixture into stew; stir. Cover and cook on HIGH 10 minutes. *Makes 4 (2½-cup) servings*

Corned Beef and Cabbage

Broccoli and Beef Pasta

Meaty Main Dishes

2 cups broccoli florets *or*
   1 package (10 ounces)
   frozen broccoli, thawed

1 onion, thinly sliced

½ teaspoon dried basil
   leaves

½ teaspoon dried oregano
   leaves

½ teaspoon dried thyme
   leaves

1 can (14½ ounces)
   Italian-style diced
   tomatoes, undrained

¾ cup beef broth

1 pound lean ground beef

2 cloves garlic, minced

2 tablespoons tomato
   paste

2 cups cooked rotini pasta

3 ounces shredded
   Cheddar cheese or
   grated Parmesan
   cheese

SLOW COOKER DIRECTIONS

Layer broccoli, onion, basil, oregano, thyme, tomatoes with juice and beef broth in slow cooker. Cover and cook on LOW 2½ hours.

Combine beef and garlic in large nonstick skillet; cook over high heat 6 to 8 minutes or until meat is no longer pink, breaking meat apart with wooden spoon. Pour off drippings. Add beef mixture to slow cooker. Cover and cook 2 hours.

Stir in tomato paste. Add pasta and cheese. Cover and cook 30 minutes or until cheese melts and mixture is heated through. Sprinkle with additional shredded cheese, if desired.
Makes 4 servings

Broccoli and Beef Pasta

Sweet and Sour Spare Ribs

4 pounds spare ribs

2 cups dry sherry or chicken broth

½ cup pineapple, mango or guava juice

⅓ cup chicken broth

2 tablespoons packed light brown sugar

2 tablespoons cider vinegar

2 tablespoons soy sauce

1 clove garlic, minced

½ teaspoon salt

¼ teaspoon black pepper

⅛ teaspoon red pepper flakes

1 tablespoon cornstarch

SLOW COOKER DIRECTIONS

1. Preheat oven to 400°F. Place ribs in foil-lined shallow roasting pan. Bake 30 minutes, turning over after 15 minutes. Remove from oven. Slice meat into 2-rib portions. Place ribs in 5-quart slow cooker. Add remaining ingredients, except cornstarch, to slow cooker.

2. Cover and cook on LOW 6 hours. Uncover and skim fat from liquid.

3. Combine cornstarch and ¼ cup liquid from slow cooker; stir until smooth. Pour mixture back into slow cooker; mix well. Cover and cook on HIGH 10 minutes or until slightly thickened.

Makes 4 servings

Italian Sausage and Vegetable Stew

1 pound hot or mild Italian sausage, cut into 1-inch pieces

1 package (16 ounces) frozen mixed vegetables (onions and green, red and yellow bell peppers)

1 can (14½ ounces) diced Italian-style tomatoes, undrained

2 medium zucchini, sliced

1 jar (4½ ounces) sliced mushrooms, drained

4 cloves garlic, minced

2 tablespoons Italian-style tomato paste

SLOW COOKER DIRECTIONS

Heat large skillet over high heat until hot. Add sausage and cook about 5 minutes or until browned. Pour off any drippings.

Combine sausage, frozen vegetables, tomatoes with juice, zucchini, mushrooms and garlic in slow cooker. Cover and cook on LOW 4 to 4½ hours or until zucchini is tender. Stir in tomato paste. Cover and cook 30 minutes or until juices have thickened.

Makes 6 (1-cup) servings

Serving Suggestion: Serve with fresh hot garlic bread.

Oniony Braised Short Ribs

2 tablespoons olive or vegetable oil

3 pounds beef chuck short ribs

1 envelope LIPTON® RECIPE SECRETS® Onion Soup Mix

3¼ cups water

¼ cup ketchup

2 tablespoons firmly packed brown sugar

2 tablespoons sherry (optional)

½ teaspoon ground ginger

1 tablespoon all-purpose flour

¼ cup water

¼ teaspoon ground black pepper

1. In 6-quart Dutch oven or saucepot, heat oil over medium-high heat and brown short ribs in two batches. Return ribs to Dutch oven.

2. Stir in soup mix combined with 3¼ cups water, ketchup, brown sugar, sherry and ginger. Bring to a boil. Reduce heat to low and simmer covered 2 hours or until ribs are tender.

3. Remove ribs to serving platter and keep warm. In Dutch oven, add flour combined with ¼ cup water and pepper. Bring to a boil over high heat. Boil, stirring occasionally, 2 minutes or until thickened. Pour sauce over ribs. Serve, if desired, with crusty bread.

Makes 4 servings

Slow Cooker Method: Place short ribs in slow cooker. Combine 2½ cups water with soup mix, ketchup, brown sugar, sherry and ginger. Pour over ribs. Cover. Cook on LOW 8 to 10 hours or until ribs are tender. Remove ribs to serving platter. Stir ¼ cup water with flour and black pepper into juices in slow cooker. Cover and cook on HIGH 15 minutes or until thickened. Pour over ribs. Serve as above.

Beef and Vegetables in Rich Burgundy Sauce

1 package (8 ounces) sliced mushrooms

1 package (8 ounces) baby carrots

1 medium green bell pepper, cut into thin strips

1 boneless chuck roast (2 ½ pounds)

1 can (10½ ounces) condensed golden mushroom soup

¼ cup dry red wine or beef broth

1 tablespoon Worcestershire sauce

1 package (1 ounce) dried onion soup mix

¼ teaspoon black pepper

2 tablespoons water

3 tablespoons cornstarch

4 cups hot cooked noodles

Chopped fresh parsley (optional)

SLOW COOKER DIRECTIONS

1. Place mushrooms, carrots and bell pepper in slow cooker. Place roast on top of vegetables. Combine soup, wine, Worcestershire sauce, soup mix and black pepper in medium bowl; mix well. Pour soup mixture over roast. Cover and cook on LOW 8 to 10 hours.

2. Blend water into cornstarch in cup until smooth; set aside. Transfer roast to cutting board; cover with foil. Let stand 10 to 15 minutes before slicing.

3. Turn slow cooker to HIGH. Stir cornstarch mixture into vegetable mixture; cover and cook 10 minutes or until thickened. Serve over cooked noodles. Garnish with parsley, if desired. *Makes 6 to 8 servings*

Beef and Vegetables in Rich Burgundy Sauce

Barbara's Pork Chop Dinner

1 tablespoon butter

1 tablespoon olive oil

6 bone-in pork loin chops

1 can (10¾ ounces) condensed cream of chicken soup, undiluted

1 can (4 ounces) mushrooms, drained and chopped

¼ cup Dijon mustard

¼ cup chicken broth

2 cloves garlic, minced

½ teaspoon salt

½ teaspoon dried basil leaves

¼ teaspoon black pepper

6 red potatoes, unpeeled, cut into thin slices

1 onion, sliced

Chopped fresh parsley

SLOW COOKER DIRECTIONS

Heat butter and oil in large skillet. Brown pork chops on both sides. Set aside.

Combine soup, mushrooms, mustard, chicken broth, garlic, salt, basil and pepper in slow cooker. Add potatoes and onion, stirring to coat. Place pork chops on top of potato mixture. Cover and cook on LOW 8 to 10 hours or on HIGH 4 to 5 hours. Sprinkle with parsley just before serving. *Makes 6 servings*

Ham and Potato Casserole

1½ pounds red potatoes, peeled and sliced

8 ounces thinly sliced ham

2 poblano chili peppers, cut into thin strips

2 tablespoons olive oil

1 tablespoon dried oregano leaves

¼ teaspoon salt

1 cup (4 ounces) shredded Monterey Jack cheese

2 tablespoons finely chopped fresh cilantro

SLOW COOKER DIRECTIONS

1. Combine all ingredients, except cheese and cilantro, in slow cooker; mix well. Cover and cook on LOW 7 hours or on HIGH 4 hours.

2. Transfer potato mixture to serving dish and sprinkle with cheese and cilantro. Let stand 3 minutes or until cheese melts. *Makes 6 to 7 servings*

Barbara's Pork Chop Dinner

Barbecued Pulled Pork

3 to 4 pound boneless pork roast (shoulder or butt)
1 teaspoon salt
1 teaspoon ground cumin
1 teaspoon paprika
1 teaspoon black pepper
½ teaspoon ground red pepper
1 medium onion, sliced
1 medium green bell pepper, sliced
1 jar (18 ounces) barbecue sauce
½ cup packed brown sugar
Cooked rice and flour tortillas (optional)

SLOW COOKER DIRECTIONS

Trim excess fat from pork. Combine salt, cumin, paprika, black pepper and ground red pepper in small bowl; rub over pork. Place onion and bell pepper in slow cooker; add pork. Combine barbecue sauce and brown sugar; pour over meat. Cover and cook on LOW 8 to 10 hours. Serve over rice with tortillas, if desired.

Makes 4 to 6 servings

Black Bean and Sausage Stew

3 cans (15 ounces each) black beans, drained and rinsed
1½ cups chopped onions
1½ cups chicken broth
1 cup sliced celery
1 cup chopped red pepper
4 cloves garlic, minced
1½ teaspoons dried oregano
¾ teaspoon ground coriander
½ teaspoon ground cumin
¼ teaspoon ground red pepper
6 ounces cooked turkey sausage, thinly sliced

SLOW COOKER DIRECTIONS

1. Combine all ingredients in slow cooker, except sausage. Cover and cook on LOW 6 to 8 hours.

2. Transfer about 1½ cups bean mixture from slow cooker to blender or food processor; purée bean mixture. Return to slow cooker. Stir in sausage. Cover and cook on LOW an additional 10 to 15 minutes.

Makes 6 servings

Barbecued Pulled Pork

Favorite Beef Stew

3 carrots, cut lengthwise into halves, then cut into 1-inch pieces

3 ribs celery, cut into 1-inch pieces

2 large potatoes, peeled and cut into ½-inch pieces

1½ cups chopped onions

3 cloves garlic, chopped

1 bay leaf

4½ teaspoons Worcestershire sauce

¾ teaspoon dried thyme leaves

¾ teaspoon dried basil leaves

½ teaspoon black pepper

2 pounds lean beef stew meat, cut into 1-inch pieces

1 can (14½ ounces) diced tomatoes, undrained

1 can (about 14 ounces) reduced-sodium beef broth

½ cup cold water

¼ cup all-purpose flour

SLOW COOKER DIRECTIONS

Layer ingredients in slow cooker in the following order: carrots, celery, potatoes, onions, garlic, bay leaf, Worcestershire sauce, thyme, basil, pepper, beef, tomatoes with juice and broth. Cover and cook on LOW 8 to 9 hours.

Remove beef and vegetables to large serving bowl; cover and keep warm. Remove and discard bay leaf. Turn slow cooker to HIGH; cover. Stir water into flour in small bowl until smooth. Add ½ cup cooking liquid; mix well. Stir flour mixture into slow cooker. Cover and cook 15 minutes or until thickened. Pour sauce over meat and vegetables. Serve immediately.

Makes 6 to 8 servings

Favorite Beef Stew

That's Italian Meat Loaf

1 can (8 ounces) tomato
  sauce, divided
1 egg, lightly beaten
½ cup chopped onion
½ cup chopped green bell
  pepper
⅓ cup dry seasoned bread
  crumbs
2 tablespoons grated
  Parmesan cheese
½ teaspoon garlic powder
¼ teaspoon black pepper
1 pound ground beef
½ pound ground pork
1 cup shredded Asiago
  cheese

SLOW COOKER DIRECTIONS

Reserve ⅓ cup tomato sauce; set aside in refrigerator. Combine remaining tomato sauce and egg in large bowl. Stir in onion, bell pepper, bread crumbs, Parmesan cheese, garlic powder and black pepper. Add ground beef and pork; mix well and shape into loaf.

Place meat loaf on foil strips (see page 5). Place in slow cooker. Cover and cook on LOW 8 to 10 hours or on HIGH 4 to 6 hours; internal temperature should read 170°F.

Spread meat loaf with reserved tomato sauce. Sprinkle with Asiago cheese. Cover and cook 15 minutes or until cheese is melted. Using foil strips, remove meat loaf from slow cooker. *Makes 8 servings*

Cajun Sausage and Rice

8 ounces kielbasa sausage,
  cut in ¼-inch slices
1 can (14½ ounces) diced
  tomatoes, undrained
1 medium onion, diced
1 medium green bell
  pepper, diced
2 ribs celery, thinly sliced
1 tablespoon chicken
  bouillon granules
1 tablespoon steak sauce
3 bay leaves
1 teaspoon sugar
¼ to ½ teaspoon hot
  pepper sauce
1 cup uncooked instant rice
½ cup water

SLOW COOKER DIRECTIONS

1. Combine sausage, tomatoes with juice, onion, bell pepper, celery, bouillon, steak sauce, bay leaves, sugar and hot pepper sauce in slow cooker. Cover and cook on LOW 8 hours or on HIGH 4 hours.

2. Remove bay leaves; stir in rice and water. Cook an additional 25 minutes on HIGH. Garnish with chopped fresh parsley, if desired. *Makes 5 servings*

That's Italian Meat Loaf

Texas-Style Barbecued Brisket

1 beef brisket (3 to
      4 pounds), cut into
      halves, if necessary, to
      fit slow cooker
3 tablespoons
      Worcestershire sauce
1 tablespoon chili powder
1 teaspoon celery salt
1 teaspoon black pepper
1 teaspoon liquid smoke
2 cloves garlic, minced
2 bay leaves
   Barbecue Sauce (recipe
      follows)

SLOW COOKER DIRECTIONS

Trim excess fat from meat and discard. Place meat in resealable plastic food storage bag. Combine Worcestershire sauce, chili powder, celery salt, pepper, liquid smoke, garlic and bay leaves in small bowl. Spread mixture on all sides of meat; seal bag. Refrigerate 24 hours.

Place meat and marinade in slow cooker. Cover and cook on LOW 7 hours. Meanwhile, prepare Barbecue Sauce.

Remove meat from slow cooker and pour juices into 2-cup measure; let stand 5 minutes. Skim fat from juices. Remove and discard bay leaves. Stir 1 cup of defatted juices into Barbecue Sauce. Discard remaining juices. Return meat and Barbecue Sauce to slow cooker. Cover and cook on LOW 1 hour or until meat is fork-tender. Remove meat to cutting board. Cut across grain into $\frac{1}{4}$-inch-thick slices. Serve with Barbecue Sauce.

Makes 10 to 12 servings

Barbecue Sauce

2 tablespoons vegetable oil
1 medium onion, chopped
2 cloves garlic, minced
1 cup ketchup
$\frac{1}{2}$ cup molasses
$\frac{1}{4}$ cup cider vinegar
2 teaspoons chili powder
$\frac{1}{2}$ teaspoon dry mustard

Heat oil in medium saucepan over medium heat. Add onion and garlic; cook until onion is tender. Add remaining ingredients. Simmer 5 minutes.

Texas-Style Barbecued Brisket

2 small sweet potatoes, peeled and cut into 2-inch pieces (about 12 ounces total)

1 package (10 ounces) frozen corn

1 package (9 ounces) frozen cut green beans

1 cup chopped onion

1¼ pounds lean pork stew meat, cut into 1-inch cubes

1 can (14½ ounces) diced tomatoes, undrained

1 cup water

1 to 2 tablespoons chili powder

½ teaspoon salt

½ teaspoon ground coriander

SLOW COOKER DIRECTIONS

Place potatoes, corn, green beans and onion in slow cooker. Top with pork. Combine tomatoes with juice, water, chili powder, salt and coriander in large bowl. Pour over pork in slow cooker. Cover and cook on LOW 7 to 9 hours. *Makes 6 servings*

Magical Tip

To chop an onion, peel the skin and cut the onion in half through the root end. Place the onion, cut side down, on a cutting board. Cut the onion into slices perpendicular to the root end, holding the onion with your fingers to keep it together. Turn the onion half and cut it crosswise. Repeat with the remaining half.

Panama Pork Stew

Poultry Pizzazz

Turkey Mushroom Stew

1 pound turkey cutlets, cut into 4×1-inch strips

1 small onion, thinly sliced

2 tablespoons minced green onion with top

½ pound mushrooms, sliced

2 to 3 tablespoons all-purpose flour

1 cup half-and-half or milk

1 teaspoon salt

1 teaspoon dried tarragon leaves

Black pepper to taste

½ cup frozen peas

½ cup sour cream (optional)

Puff pastry shells (optional)

SLOW COOKER DIRECTIONS

Layer turkey, onions and mushrooms in slow cooker. Cover and cook on LOW 4 hours. Remove turkey and vegetables to serving bowl. Turn slow cooker to HIGH.

Blend flour into half-and-half until smooth; pour into slow cooker. Add salt, tarragon and pepper to slow cooker. Return cooked vegetables and turkey to slow cooker. Stir in peas. Cover and cook 1 hour or until sauce has thickened and peas are heated through.

Stir in sour cream just before serving, if desired. Serve in puff pastry shells. *Makes 4 servings*

Turkey Mushroom Stew

Moroccan Chicken Tagine

3 pounds chicken, cut into serving pieces and skin removed

1 can (14½ ounces) diced tomatoes, undrained

2 onions, chopped

2 cups chicken broth

1 cup dried apricots, chopped

4 cloves garlic, minced

2 teaspoons ground cumin

1 teaspoon ground cinnamon

1 teaspoon ground ginger

½ teaspoon ground coriander

½ teaspoon ground red pepper

6 sprigs fresh cilantro

1 tablespoon cornstarch

1 tablespoon water

1 can (15 ounces) chick-peas, drained and rinsed

2 tablespoons chopped fresh cilantro

¼ cup slivered almonds, toasted

Hot cooked couscous or rice

SLOW COOKER DIRECTIONS

1. Place chicken in slow cooker. Combine tomatoes with juice, onions, broth, apricots, garlic, cumin, cinnamon, ginger, coriander, red pepper and cilantro sprigs in medium bowl; pour over chicken. Cover and cook on LOW 4 to 5 hours or until chicken is no longer pink in center. Remove chicken from slow cooker; place on serving dish and cover to keep warm.

2. Combine cornstarch and water in cup and stir until smooth. Stir into slow cooker. Stir in chick-peas. Cover and cook on HIGH 15 minutes or until sauce is thickened. Pour sauce over chicken. Sprinkle with chopped cilantro and almonds. Serve with couscous or rice.

Makes 4 to 6 servings

Tip: To toast almonds, heat small nonstick skillet over medium-high heat. Add almonds; cook and stir about 3 minutes or until browned. Remove from pan at once. Let cool before adding to other ingredients.

Moroccan Chicken Tagine

Campbell's® Nacho Chicken & Rice Wraps

2 cans (10¾ ounces each)
   CAMPBELL'S®
   Condensed Cheddar
   Cheese Soup

1 cup water

2 cups PACE® Chunky Salsa
   or Picante Sauce

1¼ cups *uncooked* regular
   long-grain white rice

2 pounds skinless,
   boneless chicken
   breasts, cut into cubes

10 flour tortillas (10-inch)

SLOW COOKER DIRECTIONS

1. In slow cooker mix soup, water, salsa, rice and chicken. Cover and cook on *low* 7 to 8 hours or until chicken and rice are done.

2. Spoon *about 1 cup* rice mixture down center of each tortilla.

3. Fold opposite sides of tortilla over filling. Roll up from bottom. Cut each wrap in half.

Makes 10 servings

Prep Time: 5 minutes
Cook Time: 7 to 8 hours

Tip: For firmer rice, substitute converted rice for regular.

Campbell's® Creamy Chicken & Wild Rice

2 cans (10¾ ounces each)
   CAMPBELL'S®
   Condensed Cream of
   Chicken Soup *or* 98%
   Fat Free Cream of
   Chicken Soup

1½ cups water

1 package (6 ounces)
   seasoned long grain
   and wild rice mix

4 large carrots, thickly
   sliced (about 3 cups)

8 skinless, boneless
   chicken breast halves
   (about 2 pounds)

SLOW COOKER DIRECTIONS

In slow cooker mix soup, water, rice and carrots. Add chicken and turn to coat. Cover and cook on *low* 7 to 8 hours or until chicken and rice are done.

Makes 8 servings

Prep Time: 5 minutes
Cook Time: 7 to 8 hours

*Left to right: Campbell's® Nacho Chicken
& Rice Wraps and Campbell's® Creamy
Chicken & Wild Rice*

Forty-Clove Chicken

1 frying chicken
(3 pounds), cut into
serving pieces

Salt and black pepper

1 to 2 tablespoons olive oil

¼ cup dry white wine

⅛ cup dry vermouth

2 tablespoons chopped
fresh parsley *or*
2 teaspoons dried
parsley leaves

2 teaspoons dried basil
leaves

1 teaspoon dried oregano
leaves

Pinch of red pepper
flakes

40 cloves garlic (about
2 heads*), peeled

4 ribs celery, sliced

Juice and peel of
1 lemon

Fresh herbs (optional)

*The whole garlic bulb is called a head.

SLOW COOKER DIRECTIONS

Remove skin from chicken, if desired. Sprinkle chicken with salt and pepper. Heat oil in large skillet over medium heat. Add chicken; cook 10 minutes or until browned on all sides. Remove to platter.

Combine wine, vermouth, parsley, basil, oregano and red pepper flakes in large bowl. Add garlic and celery; coat well. Transfer garlic and celery to slow cooker with slotted spoon. Add chicken to remaining herb mixture; coat well. Place chicken on top of celery in slow cooker. Sprinkle lemon juice and peel in slow cooker; add remaining herb mixture. Cover and cook on LOW 6 hours or until chicken is no longer pink in center. Garnish with fresh herbs, if desired.

Makes 4 to 6 servings

Forty-Clove Chicken

Chili Turkey Loaf

2 pounds ground turkey

1 cup chopped onion

⅔ cup Italian-style seasoned dry bread crumbs

½ cup chopped green bell pepper

½ cup chili sauce

2 eggs, slightly beaten

2 tablespoons horseradish mustard

4 cloves garlic, minced

1 teaspoon salt

½ teaspoon dried Italian seasoning

¼ teaspoon black pepper

Prepared salsa (optional)

SLOW COOKER DIRECTIONS

Make foil handles for loaf using technique described below. Mix all ingredients except salsa in large bowl. Shape into round loaf and place on foil strips. Transfer to bottom of slow cooker using foil handles. Cover and cook on LOW 4½ to 5 hours or until juices run clear and temperature is 170°F. Remove loaf from slow cooker using foil handles. Place on serving plate. Let stand 5 minutes before serving. Cut into wedges and top with salsa, if desired. Serve with steamed carrots, if desired. *Makes 8 servings*

Foil Handles: Tear off three 18×2-inch strips of heavy foil or use regular foil folded to double thickness. Crisscross foil strips in spoke design and place in slow cooker to allow for easy removal of turkey loaf.

90's-Style Slow Cooker Coq au Vin

2 packages BUTTERBALL® Boneless Skinless Chicken Breast Fillets

1 pound fresh mushrooms, sliced thick

1 jar (15 ounces) pearl onions, drained

½ cup dry white wine

1 teaspoon thyme leaves

1 bay leaf

1 cup chicken broth

⅓ cup flour

½ cup chopped fresh parsley

SLOW COOKER DIRECTIONS

Place chicken, mushrooms, onions, wine, thyme and bay leaf in slow cooker. Combine chicken broth and flour; pour into slow cooker. Cover and cook 5 hours on low setting. Add parsley. Serve over wild rice pilaf, if desired. *Makes 8 servings*

Prep Time: 30 minutes plus cooking time

Chili Turkey Loaf

Coconut Chicken Curry

1 tablespoon vegetable oil

4 boneless skinless chicken breast halves

3 medium potatoes, peeled and chopped

1 medium onion, sliced

1 can (14 ounces) coconut milk

1 cup chicken broth

1½ teaspoons curry powder

1 teaspoon hot pepper sauce (optional)

½ teaspoon salt

½ teaspoon black pepper

1 package (10 ounces) frozen peas, thawed

SLOW COOKER DIRECTIONS

1. Heat oil in medium skillet. Add chicken breasts and brown on both sides. Place potatoes and onion in slow cooker. Place chicken breasts on top. Combine coconut milk, broth, curry powder, hot sauce, if desired, salt and pepper in medium bowl. Add to slow cooker. Cover and cook on LOW 6 to 8 hours.

2. About 30 minutes before serving, add peas to slow cooker. Serve over hot cooked rice or Asian noodles, if desired. *Makes 4 servings*

Brunswick Stew

1 package (about 2 pounds) PERDUE® Fresh Chicken Thighs

2 cans (14½ ounces each) chicken broth

3 potatoes, peeled and diced into ½-inch pieces (3 cups)

1 can (14½ ounces) Cajun- or Mexican-style tomatoes

1 package (10 ounces) frozen succotash, partially thawed

Salt and ground black pepper to taste

Hot pepper sauce to taste

SLOW COOKER DIRECTIONS

In slow cooker, combine chicken, chicken broth and potatoes. Cover and cook on low heat 2½ to 3 hours, until chicken is cooked through. Add tomatoes, succotash, salt and pepper. Turn heat to high; cover and cook 1 hour. Season to taste with salt, pepper and hot pepper sauce. Serve in soup bowls.

Makes 4 to 6 servings

Note: This recipe can also be cooked in a Dutch oven on top of the stove over medium-low heat for about 1 hour. For added flavor, stir in ½ cup diced PERDUE® Turkey Ham.

Coconut Chicken Curry

3 cups chopped cooked chicken

1½ cups cottage cheese

1 can (10¾ ounces) condensed cream of chicken soup, undiluted

1 package (8 ounces) wide egg noodles, cooked and drained

1 cup grated Monterey Jack cheese

½ cup diced celery

½ cup diced onion

½ cup diced green bell pepper

½ cup diced red bell pepper

½ cup grated Parmesan cheese

½ cup chicken broth

1 can (4 ounces) sliced mushrooms, drained

2 tablespoons butter, melted

½ teaspoon dried thyme leaves

SLOW COOKER DIRECTIONS

Combine all ingredients in slow cooker. Stir to coat evenly. Cover and cook on LOW 6 to 10 hours or on HIGH 3 to 4 hours.   *Makes 6 servings*

Magical Tip

When a recipe calls for chopped cooked chicken, it can be difficult to judge how much chicken to purchase. As a guideline, two whole chicken breasts (about 10 ounces each) will yield about 2 cups of chopped cooked chicken; one broiling/frying chicken (about 3 pounds) will yield about 2½ cups chopped cooked chicken.

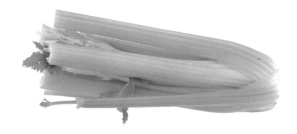

3-Cheese Chicken & Noodles

Poultry Pizzazz

COWPOKE BARBECUE SAUCE

- 1 can (8 ounces) tomato sauce
- ⅓ cup chopped green onions
- ¼ cup ketchup
- 2 tablespoons water
- 2 tablespoons orange juice
- 1 tablespoon cider vinegar
- 1 tablespoon chili sauce
- 2 cloves garlic, finely chopped
- ½ teaspoon vegetable oil
  Dash Worcestershire sauce

FAJITAS

- 10 ounces boneless skinless chicken breasts, cut lengthwise into 1 × ½-inch pieces
- 2 green or red bell peppers, thinly sliced
- 1 cup sliced onion
- 2 cups tomato wedges
- 4 (6-inch) warm flour tortillas

SLOW COOKER DIRECTIONS

Combine all Cowpoke Barbecue Sauce ingredients in slow cooker. Cover and cook on HIGH 1½ hours.

Spray large nonstick skillet with nonstick cooking spray. Add chicken and cook over medium heat until browned. Reduce slow cooker heat to LOW. Add cooked chicken, bell peppers and onion to slow cooker. Stir until well coated. Cover and cook 3 to 4 hours or until chicken is no longer pink and vegetables are tender.

Add tomatoes; cover and cook 30 to 45 minutes or until heated through. Serve with warm tortillas.

Makes 4 servings

Chicken Fajitas with Cowpoke Barbecue Sauce

Mu Shu Turkey

1 can (16 ounces) plums, drained, rinsed and pitted

½ cup orange juice

¼ cup finely chopped onion

1 tablespoon minced fresh ginger

¼ teaspoon ground cinnamon

1 pound boneless turkey breast, cut into thin strips

6 (7-inch) flour tortillas

3 cups coleslaw mix

SLOW COOKER DIRECTIONS

1. Place plums in blender or food processor. Cover and blend until almost smooth. Combine plums, orange juice, onion, ginger and cinnamon in slow cooker; mix well. Place turkey over plum mixture. Cover and cook on LOW 3 to 4 hours.

2. Remove turkey from slow cooker and divide evenly among tortillas. Spoon about 2 tablespoons plum sauce over turkey in each tortilla; top with about ½ cup coleslaw mix. Fold bottom edge of tortilla over filling; fold in sides. Roll up to completely enclose filling. Repeat with remaining tortillas. Use remaining plum sauce for dipping. *Makes 6 servings*

Country Captain Chicken

4 chicken thighs

2 tablespoons all-purpose flour

2 tablespoons vegetable oil, divided

1 cup chopped green bell pepper

1 large onion, chopped

1 rib celery chopped

1 clove garlic, minced

¼ cup chicken broth

2 cups canned or fresh crushed tomatoes

½ cup golden raisins

1½ teaspoons curry powder

1 teaspoon salt

¼ teaspoon paprika

¼ teaspoon black pepper

2 cups hot cooked rice

SLOW COOKER DIRECTIONS

1. Coat chicken with flour; set aside. Heat 1 tablespoon oil in large skillet over medium-high heat until hot. Add bell pepper, onion, celery and garlic. Cook and stir 5 minutes or until vegetables are tender. Place vegetables in slow cooker.

2. Heat remaining 1 tablespoon oil in same skillet over medium-high heat. Add chicken and cook 5 minutes per side. Place chicken in slow cooker.

3. Pour broth into skillet. Heat over medium-high heat, stirring frequently and scraping up any browned bits from bottom of skillet. Pour liquid into slow cooker. Add tomatoes, raisins, curry powder, salt, paprika and black pepper. Cover and cook on LOW 3 hours. Serve chicken with sauce over rice. *Makes 4 servings*

Mu Shu Turkey

Simple Coq au Vin

4 chicken legs
Salt and black pepper
2 tablespoons olive oil
½ pound mushrooms, sliced
1 onion, sliced into rings
½ cup red wine
½ teaspoon dried basil leaves
½ teaspoon dried thyme leaves
½ teaspoon dried oregano leaves
Hot cooked rice

SLOW COOKER DIRECTIONS

Sprinkle chicken with salt and pepper. Heat oil in large skillet; brown chicken on both sides. Remove chicken and place in slow cooker. Sauté mushrooms and onion in same skillet. Add wine; stir and scrape brown bits from bottom of skillet. Add mixture to slow cooker. Sprinkle with basil, thyme and oregano. Cover and cook on LOW 8 to 10 hours or on HIGH 3 to 4 hours.

Serve chicken and sauce over rice.   *Makes 4 servings*

Old World Chicken and Vegetables

1 tablespoon dried oregano leaves
1 teaspoon salt, divided
1 teaspoon paprika
½ teaspoon garlic powder
¼ teaspoon black pepper
2 medium green bell peppers, cut into thin strips
1 small yellow onion, thinly sliced
1 cut-up whole chicken (3 pounds)
⅓ cup ketchup
6 ounces uncooked egg noodles

SLOW COOKER DIRECTIONS

1. In small bowl, combine oregano, ½ teaspoon salt, paprika, garlic powder and black pepper; mix well.

2. Place bell peppers and onion in slow cooker. Top with chicken thighs and legs, sprinkle with half the oregano mixture, top with chicken breasts. Sprinkle chicken with remaining oregano mixture. Cover and cook on LOW 8 hours or on HIGH 4 hours. Stir in ketchup and remaining ½ teaspoon salt. Just before serving, cook noodles following package directions; drain. Serve chicken and vegetables over noodles.

Makes 4 servings

Simple Coq au Vin

Herbed Chicken & Vegetables

2 medium all-purpose potatoes, thinly sliced (about 1 pound)

2 medium carrots, sliced

4 bone-in chicken pieces (about 2 pounds)

1 envelope LIPTON® RECIPE SECRETS® Savory Herb with Garlic Soup Mix

⅓ cup water

1 tablespoon olive or vegetable oil

1. Preheat oven to 425°F. In broiler pan, without the rack, place potatoes and carrots; arrange chicken on top. Pour soup mix blended with water and oil over chicken and vegetables.

2. Bake uncovered 40 minutes or until chicken is no longer pink and vegetables are tender.

Makes 4 servings

Slow Cooker Method: Place all ingredients in slow cooker, arranging chicken on top; cover. Cook on HIGH 4 hours or LOW 6 to 8 hours.

Harvest Drums

1 package (about 1¼ pounds) PERDUE® Fresh Skinless Chicken Drumsticks

½ teaspoon dried Italian herb seasoning

Salt and ground pepper

3 bacon slices, diced

2 cans (14½ ounces each) pasta-ready tomatoes with cheeses

1 small onion, chopped

¼ cup red wine

1 clove garlic, minced

1 small zucchini, scrubbed and julienned

1 package (12 ounces) angel hair pasta, cooked and drained

Sprinkle chicken with Italian seasoning and salt and pepper to taste. In large, nonstick skillet over medium-low heat, cook bacon about 5 minutes, until crisp. Remove from skillet; drain and crumble. Increase heat to medium-high. Add chicken to bacon drippings (or replace drippings with 1½ tablespoons olive oil); cook 4 to 5 minutes on all sides or until brown, turning often.

In large slow cooker, combine tomatoes, bacon, onion, wine and garlic. Add chicken; cook on high 1½ to 1¾ hours, or until fork-tender. Add zucchini during last 5 minutes of cooking. Serve chicken and vegetables over angel hair pasta.

Makes 3 to 4 servings

Herbed Chicken & Vegetables

Pineapple Chicken and Sweet Potatoes

⅔ cup plus 3 tablespoons all-purpose flour, divided

1 teaspoon salt

1 teaspoon ground nutmeg

½ teaspoon ground cinnamon

⅛ teaspoon onion powder

⅛ teaspoon black pepper

6 chicken breasts

3 sweet potatoes, peeled and sliced

1 can (10¾ ounces) condensed cream of chicken soup, undiluted

½ cup pineapple juice

¼ pound mushrooms, sliced

2 teaspoons brown sugar

½ teaspoon grated orange peel

SLOW COOKER DIRECTIONS

Combine ⅔ cup flour, salt, nutmeg, cinnamon, onion powder and black pepper in large bowl. Thoroughly coat chicken in flour mixture. Place sweet potatoes on bottom of slow cooker. Top with chicken.

Combine soup, pineapple juice, mushrooms, remaining 3 tablespoons flour, brown sugar and orange peel in medium bowl; stir well. Pour soup mixture into slow cooker. Cover and cook on LOW 8 to 10 hours or on HIGH 3 to 4 hours. Serve chicken and sauce over hot cooked rice, if desired. *Make 6 servings*

He-Man Stew

1 package (about 3½ pounds) PERDUE® Fresh Skinless Pick of the Chicken

Salt and ground pepper

2 tablespoons olive oil

1 can (12 ounces) lite beer

1 can (28 ounces) whole plum tomatoes, drained and chopped

1 onion, sliced into rings

¼ cup spicy brown mustard

4 cups cooked elbow macaroni

SLOW COOKER DIRECTIONS

Season chicken with salt and pepper to taste. In large nonstick skillet over medium-high heat, heat oil. Add chicken; cook 5 to 6 minutes on each side for larger pieces, 3 to 4 minutes on each side for smaller pieces, or until brown, turning often. In large slow cooker, combine beer, tomatoes, onion and mustard. Add chicken. Cook on high 1½ to 2 hours, or until chicken is fork-tender. Serve over macaroni.

Makes 3 to 4 servings

Pineapple Chicken and Sweet Potatoes

Campbell's® Lemon Chicken

2 cans (10¾ ounces each) CAMPBELL'S® Condensed Cream of Chicken Soup *or* 98% Fat Free Cream of Chicken Soup

½ cup water

¼ cup lemon juice

2 teaspoons Dijon-style mustard

1½ teaspoons garlic powder

8 large carrots, thickly sliced (about 6 cups)

8 skinless, boneless chicken breast halves (about 2 pounds)

8 cups hot cooked egg noodles

Grated Parmesan cheese

SLOW COOKER DIRECTIONS

1. In slow cooker mix soup, water, lemon juice, mustard, garlic powder and carrots. Add chicken and turn to coat. Cover and cook on *low* 7 to 8 hours or until chicken is done.

2. Serve over noodles. Sprinkle with cheese.

Makes 8 servings

Prep Time: 5 minutes
Cook Time: 7 to 8 hours

Herbed Turkey Breast with Orange Sauce

1 large onion, chopped

3 cloves garlic, minced

1 teaspoon dried rosemary

½ teaspoon black pepper

2 to 3 pounds boneless, skinless turkey breast

1½ cups orange juice

SLOW COOKER DIRECTIONS

1. Place onion in slow cooker. Mix garlic, rosemary and pepper in small bowl; set aside. Cut slices in turkey about ¾ of the way through turkey breast at 2-inch intervals. Stuff slices with herb mixture.

2. Place turkey in slow cooker. Pour orange juice over turkey. Cover and cook on LOW 7 to 8 hours or until turkey is no longer pink in center.

Makes 4 to 6 servings

Left to right: Campbell's® Lemon Chicken and Campbell's® Asian Tomato Beef (page 50)

Sweet Chicken Curry

1 pound boneless skinless chicken breast, cut into 1-inch pieces

1 large green or red bell pepper, cut into 1-inch pieces

1 large onion, sliced

1 large tomato, seeded and chopped

$\frac{1}{2}$ cup prepared mango chutney

$\frac{1}{4}$ cup water

2 tablespoons cornstarch

$1\frac{1}{2}$ teaspoons curry powder

$1\frac{1}{3}$ cups hot cooked rice

SLOW COOKER DIRECTIONS

1. Place chicken, bell pepper and onion in slow cooker. Top with tomato. Mix chutney, water, cornstarch and curry powder in small bowl.

2. Pour chutney mixture over chicken mixture in slow cooker. Cover and cook on LOW $3\frac{1}{2}$ to $4\frac{1}{2}$ hours. Serve over rice.   *Makes 4 servings*

Easy Weeknight Chicken Cacciatore

1 tablespoon olive or vegetable oil

$2\frac{1}{2}$ pounds chicken pieces

1 package (8 ounces) fresh mushrooms, sliced

1 can (28 ounces) crushed tomatoes

1 envelope LIPTON® RECIPE SECRETS® Onion Soup Mix

$\frac{1}{4}$ cup dry red wine

$\frac{1}{2}$ teaspoon dried basil

1. In 6-quart saucepot, heat oil over medium-high heat and brown chicken pieces. Add mushrooms and cook 2 minutes, stirring occasionally.

2. Stir in crushed tomatoes, soup mix, wine and basil. Bring to a boil over high heat.

3. Reduce heat to low and simmer covered 30 minutes or until chicken is no longer pink. Serve, if desired, over hot cooked noodles or rice.   *Makes 4 servings*

Slow Cooker Method: Place mushrooms then chicken pieces in slow cooker. Stir crushed tomatoes, soup mix, wine and basil together until blended. Pour over chicken and mushrooms. Cover. Cook on HIGH 4 to 6 hours or LOW 8 hours. Serve as above.

Sweet Chicken Curry

Home-Style Sides

Mediterranean Red Potatoes

2 medium red potatoes, cut in half lengthwise then crosswise into pieces

⅔ cup fresh or frozen pearl onions

Nonstick garlic-flavored cooking spray

¾ teaspoon dried Italian seasoning

¼ teaspoon black pepper

1 small tomato, seeded and chopped

2 ounces feta cheese, crumbled

2 tablespoons chopped black olives

SLOW COOKER DIRECTIONS

1. Place potatoes and onions in $1\frac{1}{2}$-quart soufflé dish. Spray potatoes and onions with cooking spray; toss to coat. Add Italian seasoning and pepper; mix well. Cover dish tightly with foil.

2. Tear off 3 (18×3-inch) strips of heavy-duty aluminum foil. Cross strips to resemble wheel spokes. Place soufflé dish in center of strips. Pull foil strips up and over dish and place dish into slow cooker.

3. Pour hot water to about $1\frac{1}{2}$ inches from top of soufflé dish. Cover and cook on LOW 7 to 8 hours.

4. Use foil handles to lift dish out of slow cooker. Stir tomato, feta cheese and olives into potato mixture.

Makes 4 servings

Mediterranean Red Potatoes

Spicy Beans Tex-Mex

⅓ cup lentils

1⅓ cups water

5 strips bacon

1 onion, chopped

1 can (16 ounces) pinto beans, undrained

1 can (16 ounces) red kidney beans, undrained

1 can (15 ounces) diced tomatoes, undrained

3 tablespoons ketchup

3 cloves garlic, minced

1 teaspoon chili powder

½ teaspoon ground cumin

¼ teaspoon red pepper flakes

1 bay leaf

SLOW COOKER DIRECTIONS

Boil lentils in water 20 to 30 minutes in large saucepan; drain. In small skillet, cook bacon until crisp; remove, drain and crumble bacon. In same skillet, cook onion in bacon drippings until soft. Combine lentils, bacon, onion, beans with juice, tomatoes with juice, ketchup, garlic, chili powder, cumin, pepper flakes and bay leaf in slow cooker. Cook on HIGH 3 to 4 hours. Remove bay leaf before serving. *Makes 8 to 10 servings*

Spinach Spoonbread

1 package (10 ounces) frozen chopped spinach, thawed and squeezed dry

1 red bell pepper, seeded and diced

4 eggs, lightly beaten

1 cup cottage cheese

1 package (5½ ounces) cornbread mix

6 green onions, sliced

½ cup butter, melted

1¼ teaspoons seasoned salt

SLOW COOKER DIRECTIONS

1. Combine all ingredients in large bowl; mix well.

2. Pour batter into oiled, preheated slow cooker. Cook, covered, with lid slightly ajar to allow excess moisture to escape, on HIGH 1¾ to 2 hours or on LOW 3 to 4 hours or until edges are golden and knife inserted in center of bread comes out clean.

3. Serve bread spooned from slow cooker, or loosen edges and bottom with knife and invert onto plate. Cut into wedges to serve. *Makes 8 servings*

Spicy Beans Tex-Mex

Cran-Orange Acorn Squash

3 small carnival or acorn squash

5 tablespoons instant brown rice

3 tablespoons dried cranberries

3 tablespoons diced celery

3 tablespoons minced onion

Pinch ground or dried sage

1 teaspoon butter, divided

3 tablespoons orange juice

½ cup water

SLOW COOKER DIRECTIONS

1. Slice off tops and bottoms of squash. Scoop out seeds and discard; set squash aside.

2. Combine rice, cranberries, celery, onion and sage in small bowl. Stuff squash with rice mixture; dot with butter. Pour 1 tablespoon orange juice into each squash over stuffing. Stand squash in slow cooker. Pour water into bottom of slow cooker.

3. Cover; cook on LOW about 2½ hours.

Makes 6 servings

Tip: Squash can defy even the sharpest knives. To make slicing easier, microwave the whole squash on HIGH about 5 minutes to soften the skin.

Easy Dirty Rice

½ pound Italian sausage or Italian turkey sausage

2 cups water

1 large onion, finely chopped

1 large green bell pepper, finely chopped

1 cup uncooked long-grain rice

½ cup finely chopped celery

1½ teaspoons salt

½ teaspoon ground red pepper

½ cup chopped fresh parsley

SLOW COOKER DIRECTIONS

Remove casing from sausage. Cook sausage in skillet, stirring to break up meat, until no longer pink. Place cooked sausage in slow cooker. Add all remaining ingredients except parsley. Stir to combine. Cover and cook on LOW 2 hours or until rice is tender. Stir in parsley.

Makes 4 servings

Cran-Orange Acorn Squash

Broccoli & Cheese Strata

2 cups chopped broccoli
    florets
4 slices firm white bread,
    ½-inch thick
4 teaspoons butter
1½ cups (6 ounces)
    shredded Cheddar
    cheese
3 eggs
1½ cups low-fat (1%) milk
½ teaspoon salt
½ teaspoon hot pepper
    sauce
⅛ teaspoon black pepper

SLOW COOKER DIRECTIONS

1. Cook broccoli in boiling water 10 minutes or until tender. Drain. Spread one side of each bread slice with 1 teaspoon butter.

2. Arrange 2 slices bread, buttered sides up, in greased 1-quart casserole that will fit in slow cooker. Layer cheese, broccoli and remaining 2 bread slices, buttered sides down.

3. Beat eggs, milk, salt, hot pepper sauce and black pepper in medium bowl. Gradually pour over bread.

4. Place small wire rack in 5-quart slow cooker. Pour in 1 cup water. Place casserole on rack. Cover and cook on HIGH 3 hours. *Makes 4 servings*

Pesto Rice and Beans

1 can (15 ounces) Great
    Northern beans, rinsed
    and drained
1 can (14 ounces) chicken
    broth
¾ cup uncooked long-grain
    white rice
1½ cups frozen cut green
    beans, thawed and
    drained
½ cup prepared pesto
    Grated Parmesan cheese
    (optional)

SLOW COOKER DIRECTIONS

Combine Great Northern beans, chicken broth and rice in slow cooker. Cover and cook on LOW 2 hours.

Stir in green beans; cover and cook 1 hour or until rice and beans are tender. Turn off slow cooker and remove insert to heatproof surface. Stir in pesto and Parmesan cheese, if desired. Let stand, covered, 5 minutes or until cheese is melted. Serve immediately.

Makes 8 servings

Broccoli & Cheese Strata

Hearty Lentil Stew

1 cup dried lentils, rinsed
   and drained

1 package (16 ounces)
   frozen green beans

2 cups cauliflower florets

1 cup chopped onion

1 cup baby carrots, cut in
   half crosswise

3 cups fat-free reduced-
   sodium chicken broth

2 teaspoons ground cumin

¾ teaspoon ground ginger

1 can (15 ounces) chunky
   tomato sauce with
   garlic and herbs

½ cup dry-roasted peanuts

SLOW COOKER DIRECTIONS

1. Place lentils in slow cooker. Top with green beans, cauliflower, onion and carrots. Combine broth, cumin and ginger in large bowl; mix well. Pour mixture over vegetables. Cover and cook on LOW 9 to 11 hours.

2. Stir in tomato sauce. Cover and cook on LOW 10 minutes. Ladle stew into bowls. Sprinkle peanuts evenly over each serving.   *Makes 6 servings*

Rustic Garlic Mashed Potatoes

2 pounds baking potatoes,
   unpeeled and cut into
   ½-inch cubes

¼ cup water

2 tablespoons butter, cut in
   ⅛-inch pieces

1¼ teaspoons salt

½ teaspoon garlic powder

¼ teaspoon black pepper

1 cup milk

SLOW COOKER DIRECTIONS

Place all ingredients, except milk, in slow cooker; toss to combine. Cover and cook on LOW 7 hours or on HIGH 4 hours. Add milk to slow cooker. Mash potatoes with potato masher or electric mixer until smooth.   *Makes 5 servings*

Hearty Lentil Stew

Sweet-Spiced Sweet Potatoes

2 pounds sweet potatoes, peeled and cut into ½-inch pieces

¼ cup packed dark brown sugar

1 teaspoon ground cinnamon

½ teaspoon ground nutmeg

⅛ teaspoon salt

2 tablespoons butter, cut into ⅛-inch pieces

1 teaspoon vanilla

SLOW COOKER DIRECTIONS

Combine all ingredients, except butter and vanilla, in slow cooker; mix well. Cover and cook on LOW 7 hours or cook on HIGH 4 hours. Add butter and vanilla; stir to blend.

Makes 4 servings

Honey Whole-Grain Bread

3 cups whole wheat bread flour, divided

2 cups warm (not hot) whole milk

¾ to 1 cup all-purpose unbleached flour, divided

¼ cup honey

2 tablespoons canola oil

1 package active dry yeast

¾ teaspoon salt

SLOW COOKER DIRECTIONS

1. Spray 1-quart casserole, soufflé dish or other high-sided baking pan with nonstick cooking spray. Combine 1½ cups whole wheat flour, milk, ½ cup all-purpose flour, honey, oil, yeast and salt in large bowl. Beat at low speed of electric mixer 2 minutes.

2. Add remaining 1½ cups whole wheat flour and ¼ cup to ½ cup all-purpose flour. If mixer has difficulty mixing dough, mix in remaining flours with wooden spoon. Transfer to prepared dish. Place dish in slow cooker; cover and cook on HIGH about 3 hours or until edges are browned.

3. Remove from slow cooker. Let stand 5 minutes. Unmold on wire rack to cool.

Makes 8 to 10 servings

Sweet-Spiced Sweet Potatoes

Vegetable Pasta Sauce

2 cans (14½ ounces each) diced tomatoes, undrained

1 can (14½ ounces) whole tomatoes, undrained

1½ cups sliced mushrooms

1 medium red bell pepper, diced

1 medium green bell pepper, diced

1 small zucchini, cut into ¼-inch slices

1 small yellow squash, cut into ¼-inch slices

1 can (6 ounces) tomato paste

4 green onions, sliced

2 tablespoons dried Italian seasoning

1 tablespoon chopped fresh parsley

3 cloves garlic, minced

1 teaspoon salt

1 teaspoon red pepper flakes (optional)

1 teaspoon black pepper

Cooked pasta

Parmesan cheese and fresh basil for garnish (optional)

SLOW COOKER DIRECTIONS

Combine all ingredients except pasta and garnishes in slow cooker, stirring thoroughly to combine. Cover and cook on LOW 6 to 8 hours. Serve over cooked pasta. Garnish with Parmesan cheese and fresh basil, if desired.

Makes 4 to 6 servings

Magical Tip

The most familiar sweet pepper is the green pepper, also known as the bell pepper for its bell-like shape. Green peppers are picked before they ripen. When ripe, a bell pepper is red, yellow, orange, white or purple, depending on the variety. They tend to be sweeter and crisper than green peppers.

Vegetable Pasta Sauce

Swiss Cheese Scalloped Potatoes

2 pounds baking potatoes, peeled and thinly sliced

½ cup finely chopped yellow onion

¼ teaspoon salt

¼ teaspoon ground nutmeg

2 tablespoons butter, cut into ⅛-inch pieces

½ cup milk

2 tablespoons all-purpose flour

3 ounces Swiss cheese slices, torn into small pieces

¼ cup finely chopped green onions (optional)

SLOW COOKER DIRECTIONS

1. Layer half the potatoes, ¼ cup onion, ⅛ teaspoon salt, ⅛ teaspoon nutmeg and 1 tablespoon butter in slow cooker. Repeat layers. Cover and cook on LOW 7 hours or on HIGH 4 hours. Remove potatoes with slotted spoon to serving dish.

2. Blend milk and flour in small bowl until smooth. Stir mixture into slow cooker. Add cheese; stir to combine. If slow cooker is on LOW, turn to HIGH, cover and cook until slightly thickened, about 10 minutes. Stir. Pour cheese mixture over potatoes and serve. Garnish with chopped green onions, if desired.

Makes 5 to 6 servings

Swiss Cheese Scalloped Potatoes

Green Bean Casserole

- 2 packages (10 ounces each) frozen green beans, thawed
- 1 can (10½ ounces) condensed cream of mushroom soup, undiluted
- 1 tablespoon chopped fresh parsley
- 1 tablespoon chopped roasted red peppers
- 1 teaspoon dried sage
- ½ teaspoon salt
- ½ teaspoon black pepper
- ¼ teaspoon ground nutmeg
- ½ cup toasted slivered almonds

SLOW COOKER DIRECTIONS

Combine all ingredients except almonds in slow cooker. Cover and cook on LOW 3 to 4 hours. Sprinkle with almonds.   *Makes 4 to 6 servings*

Skinny Cornbread

- 1¼ cups all-purpose flour
- ¾ cup yellow cornmeal
- ¼ cup sugar
- 1 teaspoon baking powder
- 1 teaspoon baking soda
- 1 teaspoon seasoned salt
- 1 cup nonfat buttermilk
- ¼ cup cholesterol-free egg substitute
- ¼ cup canola oil

SLOW COOKER DIRECTIONS

Sift together flour, cornmeal, sugar, baking powder, baking soda and seasoned salt in large bowl. Make well in center of dry mixture. Pour in buttermilk, egg substitute and oil. Mix in dry ingredients just until moistened. Pour mixture into oiled 2-quart soufflé dish or 2-pound coffee can. Cover with lid or foil. Place on rack in preheated slow cooker. Cook on HIGH 30 minutes to 2 hours or on LOW 3 to 4 hours or until edges are golden and knife inserted in center comes out clean.   *Makes 8 servings*

Note: You may wish to cook the cornbread with slow cooker lid slightly ajar to allow any condensation to evaporate.

Green Bean Casserole

Orange-Spice Glazed Carrots

1 package (32 ounces)
  baby carrots
½ cup packed light brown
  sugar
½ cup orange juice
3 tablespoons butter or
  margarine
¾ teaspoon ground
  cinnamon
¼ teaspoon ground nutmeg
2 tablespoons cornstarch
¼ cup cold water

SLOW COOKER DIRECTIONS

Combine all ingredients except cornstarch and water in slow cooker. Cover and cook on LOW 3½ to 4 hours or until carrots are crisp-tender. Spoon carrots into serving bowl. Remove juices to small saucepan. Heat to a boil. Mix cornstarch and water in small bowl until blended. Stir into saucepan. Boil 1 minute or until thickened, stirring constantly. Spoon over carrots.

Makes 6 servings

Scalloped Potatoes and Parsnips

6 tablespoons unsalted
  butter
3 tablespoons all-purpose
  flour
1¾ cup heavy cream
2 teaspoons dry mustard
1½ teaspoons salt
1 teaspoon dried thyme
  leaves
½ teaspoon black pepper
2 baking potatoes, cut in
  half lengthwise, then in
  ¼-inch slices crosswise
2 parsnips, cut into ¼-inch
  slices
1 onion, chopped
2 cups shredded sharp
  Cheddar cheese

SLOW COOKER DIRECTIONS

1. Melt butter in saucepan over medium-high heat. Add flour and whisk constantly for 3 to 5 minutes. Slowly whisk in cream, mustard, salt, thyme and pepper. Stir until smooth.

2. Place potatoes, parsnips and onion in slow cooker. Add cream sauce and carefully combine. Cover and cook on LOW 7 hours or on HIGH 3½ hours or until potatoes are tender. Stir in cheese. Cover until cheese melts.

Makes 4 to 6 servings

Orange-Spice Glazed Carrots

Asparagus and Cheese Side Dish

1 ½ pounds fresh asparagus, trimmed

2 cups crushed saltine crackers

1 can (10¾ ounces) condensed cream of asparagus soup, undiluted

1 can (10¾ ounces) condensed cream of chicken soup, undiluted

⅔ cup slivered almonds

¼ pound American cheese, cut into cubes

1 egg

SLOW COOKER DIRECTIONS

Combine all ingredients in large bowl; stir well. Pour into slow cooker. Cover and cook on HIGH 3 to 3 ½ hours.   *Makes 4 to 6 servings*

Magical Tip

Store asparagus upright with the stems in a few inches of water. Or, wrap it in damp paper towels and place in a plastic bag. For the best flavor, refrigerate asparagus as soon as possible and use it within one or two days.

New England Baked Beans

4 slices uncooked bacon, chopped

3 cans (15 ounces each) Great Northern beans, rinsed and drained

¾ cup water

1 small onion, chopped

⅓ cup canned diced tomatoes, well drained

3 tablespoons packed light brown sugar

3 tablespoons maple syrup

3 tablespoons unsulphured molasses

2 cloves garlic, minced

½ teaspoon salt

½ teaspoon dry mustard

⅛ teaspoon black pepper

½ bay leaf

SLOW COOKER DIRECTIONS

Cook bacon in large skillet until almost cooked but not crispy. Drain on paper towels.

Combine bacon and all remaining ingredients in slow cooker. Cover and cook on LOW 6 to 8 hours or until onion is tender and mixture is thickened. Remove bay leaf before serving.   *Makes 4 to 6 servings*

Asparagus and Cheese Side Dish

Garden Potato Casserole

1 ¼ pounds baking potatoes, unpeeled and sliced

1 small green or red bell pepper, thinly sliced

¼ cup finely chopped yellow onion

2 tablespoons butter, cut into ⅛-inch pieces, divided

½ teaspoon salt

½ teaspoon dried thyme leaves

Black pepper to taste

1 small yellow squash, thinly sliced

1 cup (4 ounces) shredded sharp Cheddar cheese

SLOW COOKER DIRECTIONS

1. Place potatoes, bell pepper, onion, 1 tablespoon butter, salt, thyme and black pepper in slow cooker; mix well. Layer squash evenly on top in slow cooker; sprinkle with remaining 1 tablespoon butter. Cover and cook on LOW 7 hours or on HIGH 4 hours.

2. Remove potato mixture to serving bowl. Sprinkle with cheese and let stand 2 to 3 minutes or until cheese melts. *Makes 5 servings*

Magical Tip

Store potatoes in a cool, dry dark place (light and warmth encourage sprouting) for up to two weeks. Avoid storing potatoes and onions together as the gases given off by the onions can cause the potatoes to spoil more quickly. Avoid storing potatoes in the refrigerator as the starch turns to sugar making them overly sweet.

Garden Potato Casserole

Red Cabbage and Apples

1 small red cabbage, cored
   and thinly sliced

3 medium apples, peeled,
   cored and grated

¾ cup sugar

½ cup red wine vinegar

1 teaspoon ground cloves

1 cup cooked crumbled
   bacon (optional)

SLOW COOKER DIRECTIONS

Combine cabbage, apples, sugar, red wine vinegar
and cloves in slow cooker. Cover and cook on HIGH
6 hours, stirring after 3 hours. Sprinkle with bacon, if
desired. *Makes 4 to 6 servings*

Sunshine Squash

1 butternut squash (about
   2 pounds) peeled,
   seeded and diced

1 can (about 15 ounces)
   kernel corn, drained

1 can (14½ ounces)
   tomatoes, undrained

1 medium onion, coarsely
   chopped

1 green bell pepper,
   seeded and cut into
   1-inch pieces

½ cup chicken broth

1 canned green chili,
   coarsely chopped

1 clove garlic, minced

½ teaspoon salt

¼ teaspoon black pepper

1 tablespoon plus
   1½ teaspoons tomato
   paste

SLOW COOKER DIRECTIONS

Combine all ingredients except tomato paste in slow
cooker. Cover and cook on LOW 6 hours or until
squash is tender.

Remove about ¼ cup cooking liquid and blend with
tomato paste. Stir into slow cooker. Cook 30 minutes
or until mixture is slightly thickened and heated
through. *Makes 6 to 8 servings*

Red Cabbage and Apples

Delicious Desserts

Chocolate Croissant Pudding

1 ½ cups milk

3 eggs

½ cup sugar

¼ cup unsweetened cocoa powder

½ teaspoon vanilla

¼ teaspoon salt

2 plain croissants, cut into 1-inch pieces.

½ cup chocolate chips

¾ cup whipped cream (optional)

SLOW COOKER DIRECTIONS

1. Beat milk, eggs, sugar, cocoa, vanilla and salt in medium bowl.

2. Grease 1-quart casserole. Layer half the croissants, chocolate chips and half the egg mixture in casserole. Repeat layers with remaining croissants and egg mixture.

3. Add rack to 5-quart slow cooker and pour in 1 cup water. Place casserole on rack. Cover and cook on LOW 3 to 4 hours. Remove casserole from slow cooker. Top each serving with 2 tablespoons whipped cream, if desired. *Makes 6 servings*

Chocolate Croissant Pudding

Coconut Rice Pudding

2 cups water

1 cup uncooked long-grain rice

1 tablespoon unsalted butter

Pinch salt

18 ounces evaporated milk

14 ounces cream of coconut

½ cup golden raisins

3 egg yolks, beaten

Peel of 2 limes

1 teaspoon vanilla extract

Toasted shredded coconut (optional)

SLOW COOKER DIRECTIONS

1. Place water, rice, butter and salt in medium saucepan. Bring to a roiling boil over high heat, stirring frequently. Reduce heat to low. Cover and cook 10 to 12 minutes. Remove from heat. Cover and let stand 5 minutes.

2. Meanwhile, spray slow cooker with nonstick cooking spray. Add milk, cream of coconut, raisins, egg yolks, lime peel and vanilla extract; mix well. Add rice mixture; stir to combine. Cover and cook on LOW 4 hours or on HIGH 2 hours. Stir every 30 minutes, if possible. Pudding will thicken as it cools. Garnish with toasted shredded coconut, if desired.

Makes 6 (¾-cup) servings

Pear Crunch

1 can (8 ounces) crushed pineapple in juice, undrained

¼ cup pineapple or apple juice

3 tablespoons dried cranberries

1½ teaspoons quick-cooking tapioca

¼ teaspoon vanilla

2 pears, cored and cut into halves

¼ cup granola with almonds

SLOW COOKER DIRECTIONS

Combine all ingredients, except pears and granola, in slow cooker; mix well. Place pears, cut side down, over pineapple mixture. Cover and cook on LOW 3½ to 4½ hours. Arrange pear halves on serving plates. Spoon pineapple mixture over pear halves. Garnish with granola.

Makes 4 servings

Coconut Rice Pudding

Banana-Rum Custard with Vanilla Wafers

1 ½ cups milk

3 eggs

½ cup sugar

3 tablespoons dark rum or milk

⅛ teaspoon salt

1 medium banana, sliced ¼ inch thick

15 to 18 vanilla wafers

SLOW COOKER DIRECTIONS

1. Beat milk, eggs, sugar, rum and salt in medium bowl. Pour into 1-quart casserole. Do not cover.

2. Add rack to 5-quart slow cooker and pour in 1 cup water. Place casserole on rack. Cover and cook on LOW 3½ to 4 hours. Remove casserole from slow cooker. Spoon custard into individual dessert dishes, if desired. Arrange banana slices and wafers over custard. Garnish as desired. *Makes 5 servings*

Spiced Apple & Cranberry Compote

2 ½ cups cranberry juice cocktail

1 package (6 ounces) dried apples

½ cup (2 ounces) dried cranberries

½ cup Rhine wine or apple juice

½ cup honey

2 cinnamon sticks, broken into halves

Frozen yogurt or ice cream (optional)

Additional cinnamon sticks (optional)

SLOW COOKER DIRECTIONS

Mix juice, apples, cranberries, wine, honey and cinnamon stick halves in slow cooker. Cover and cook on LOW 4 to 5 hours or until liquid is absorbed and fruit is tender. Remove and discard cinnamon stick halves. Ladle compote into bowls. Serve warm, at room temperature, or chilled with scoop of frozen yogurt or ice cream, and garnish with additional cinnamon sticks, if desired. *Makes 6 servings*

Banana-Rum Custard with Vanilla Wafers

Apple-Date Crisp

6 cups thinly sliced peeled apples (about 6 medium apples, preferably Golden Delicious)

2 teaspoons lemon juice

⅓ cup chopped dates

1 ⅓ cups quick-cooking oats

½ cup all-purpose unbleached flour

½ cup packed light brown sugar

½ teaspoon ground cinnamon

¼ teaspoon ground ginger

¼ teaspoon salt

Pinch ground nutmeg

Pinch ground cloves (optional)

¼ cup (4 tablespoons) cold butter, cut into small pieces

SLOW COOKER DIRECTIONS

1. Spray slow cooker with nonstick cooking spray.

2. Place apples in large bowl. Sprinkle with lemon juice and toss well. Stir in dates. Transfer apple mixture to slow cooker.

3. Combine oats, flour, brown sugar, cinnamon, ginger, salt, nutmeg and cloves, if desired, in medium bowl. Cut in butter with pastry blender or two knives until mixture resembles coarse crumbs.

4. Pour oat mixture into slow cooker over apples; smooth top. Cover; cook on HIGH about 2 hours, or on LOW about 4 hours. *Makes 6 servings*

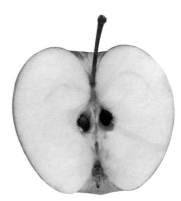

Apple-Date Crisp

Poached Pears with Raspberry Sauce

4 cups cran-raspberry juice cocktail

2 cups Rhine or Riesling wine

¼ cup sugar

2 cinnamon sticks, broken into halves

4 to 5 firm Bosc or Anjou pears, peeled and cored

1 package (10 ounces) frozen raspberries in syrup, thawed

Fresh berries (optional)

SLOW COOKER DIRECTIONS

Combine juice, wine, sugar and cinnamon stick halves in slow cooker. Submerge pears in mixture. Cover and cook on LOW 3½ to 4 hours or until pears are tender. Remove and discard cinnamon sticks.

Process raspberries in food processor or blender until smooth; strain and discard seeds. Spoon raspberry sauce onto serving plates; place pear on top of sauce. Garnish with fresh berries, if desired. *Makes 4 to 5 servings*

Cherry Rice Pudding

1½ cups milk

1 cup hot cooked rice

3 eggs, beaten

½ cup sugar

¼ cup dried cherries or cranberries

½ teaspoon almond extract

¼ teaspoon salt

SLOW COOKER DIRECTIONS

Combine all ingredients in large bowl. Pour mixture into greased 1½-quart casserole. Cover with foil. Add rack to 5-quart slow cooker and pour in 1 cup water. Place casserole on rack. Cover and cook on LOW 4 to 5 hours. Remove casserole from slow cooker. Let stand 15 minutes before serving. *Makes 6 servings*

Poached Pears with Raspberry Sauce

Pumpkin-Cranberry Custard

1 can (30 ounces) pumpkin
   pie filling
1 can (12 ounces)
   evaporated milk
1 cup dried cranberries
4 eggs, beaten
1 cup crushed or whole
   ginger snap cookies
   (optional)
Whipped cream (optional)

SLOW COOKER DIRECTIONS
Combine pumpkin, evaporated milk, cranberries, and eggs in slow cooker and mix thoroughly. Cover and cook on HIGH 4 to 4½ hours. Serve with crushed or whole ginger snaps and whipped cream, if desired.

Make 4 to 6 servings

Luscious Pecan Bread Pudding

3 cups French bread cubes
3 tablespoons chopped
   pecans, toasted
2¼ cups low-fat milk
2 eggs, beaten
½ cup sugar
1 teaspoon vanilla
¾ teaspoon ground
   cinnamon, divided
¾ cup reduced-calorie
   cranberry juice cocktail
1½ cups frozen pitted tart
   cherries
2 tablespoons sugar
   substitute

SLOW COOKER DIRECTIONS
1. Toss bread cubes and pecans in soufflé dish. Combine milk, eggs, sugar, vanilla and ½ teaspoon cinnamon in large bowl. Pour over bread mixture in soufflé dish. Cover tightly with foil. Make foil handles (see page 5). Place soufflé dish in slow cooker. Pour hot water into slow cooker to come about 1½ inches from top of soufflé dish. Cover and cook on LOW 2 to 3 hours.

2. Meanwhile, stir together cranberry juice and remaining ¼ teaspoon cinnamon in small saucepan; stir in frozen cherries. Bring sauce to a boil over medium heat, about 5 minutes. Remove from heat. Stir in sugar substitute. Lift dish from slow cooker with foil handles. Serve bread pudding with cherry sauce.

Makes 6 servings

Pumpkin-Cranberry Custard

Chocolate Chip Lemon Loaf

¾ **cup granulated sugar**

½ **cup vegetable shortening**

2 **eggs, lightly beaten**

1⅔ **cups all-purpose flour**

1½ **teaspoons baking powder**

¼ **teaspoon salt**

¾ **cup milk**

½ **cup chocolate chips**

Peel of 1 lemon

Juice of 1 lemon

¼ **to** ½ **cup powdered sugar**

Melted chocolate (optional)

SLOW COOKER DIRECTIONS

1. Grease 2-quart soufflé dish or 2-pound coffee can; set aside. Beat granulated sugar and shortening until blended. Add eggs, one at a time, mixing well after each addition.

2. Sift together flour, baking powder and salt. Add flour mixture and milk alternately to shortening mixture. Stir in chocolate chips and lemon peel.

3. Spoon batter into prepared dish. Cover with greased foil. Place in preheated slow cooker. Cook, covered, with slow cooker lid slightly ajar to allow excess moisture to escape, on HIGH 1¾ to 2 hours or on LOW 3 to 4 hours or until edges are golden and knife inserted in center of loaf comes out clean. Remove dish from slow cooker; remove foil. Place loaf on wire rack to cool completely.

4. Combine lemon juice and ¼ cup powdered sugar in small bowl. Add more sugar as needed to reach desired sweetness. Pour glaze over loaf. Drizzle loaf with melted chocolate, if desired. *Makes 8 servings*

Chocolate Chip Lemon Loaf

"Peachy Keen" Dessert Treat

1 ⅓ cups uncooked old-fashioned oats

1 cup granulated sugar

1 cup packed light brown sugar

⅔ cup buttermilk baking mix

2 teaspoons ground cinnamon

½ teaspoon ground nutmeg

2 pounds fresh peaches (about 8 medium), sliced

SLOW COOKER DIRECTIONS

Combine oats, sugars, baking mix, cinnamon and nutmeg in large bowl. Stir in peaches; mix until well blended. Pour mixture into slow cooker. Cover and cook on LOW 4 to 6 hours.   *Makes 8 to 12 servings*

Warm Spiced Apples and Pears

8 tablespoons unsalted butter

1 vanilla bean

1 cup packed dark brown sugar

½ cup water

½ lemon, sliced and seeds removed

1 cinnamon stick, broken in half

½ teaspoon ground cloves

5 pears, cored and quartered

5 small Granny Smith apples, cored and quartered

SLOW COOKER DIRECTIONS

1. Melt butter in saucepan over medium heat. Cut vanilla bean in half and scrape out seeds; add seeds and pod to pan with brown sugar, water, lemon slices, cinnamon stick and cloves. Bring to a boil; cook and stir 1 minute. Remove from heat.

2. Place pears and apples in slow cooker; pour lemon syrup over fruit and mix well. Cover and cook on LOW 3½ to 4 hours or on HIGH 2 hours. Stir apples and pears every 45 minutes to ensure even cooking.

Makes 6 servings

Serving Suggestions: Serve alone or with whipped cream, crème anglaise, sponge cake, pound cake or over ice cream. This also would pair well with baked ham, pork loin roast, or roast turkey.

"Peachy Keen" Dessert Treat

Peach Cobbler

2 packages (16 ounces each) frozen peaches, thawed and drained

¾ cup plus 1 tablespoon sugar, divided

2 teaspoons ground cinnamon, divided

½ teaspoon ground nutmeg

¾ cup all-purpose flour

6 tablespoons butter, cut into small pieces

SLOW COOKER DIRECTIONS

Combine peaches, ¾ cup sugar, 1½ teaspoons cinnamon and nutmeg in medium bowl. Place peach mixture in slow cooker. For topping, combine flour, remaining 1 tablespoon sugar and remaining ½ teaspoon cinnamon. Cut in butter with pastry cutter or two knives until mixture resembles coarse crumbs. Sprinkle over peach mixture. Cover and cook on HIGH 2 hours.

Makes 4 to 6 servings

Whole-Grain Banana Bread

¼ cup plus 2 tablespoons wheat germ, divided

⅔ cup butter, softened

1 cup sugar

2 eggs

1 cup mashed bananas (2 to 3 bananas)

1 teaspoon vanilla

1 cup whole wheat pastry flour

1 cup all-purpose flour

1 teaspoon baking soda

½ teaspoon salt

½ cup chopped walnuts or pecans (optional)

SLOW COOKER DIRECTIONS

1. Spray 1-quart casserole, soufflé dish or other high-sided baking pan with nonstick cooking spray. Sprinkle pan with 2 tablespoons wheat germ.

2. Beat butter in large bowl until fluffy. Gradually beat in sugar and eggs. Add mashed bananas and vanilla; beat until smooth.

3. Gradually stir in flours, remaining ¼ cup wheat germ, baking soda and salt. Stir in nuts, if desired. Pour batter into prepared dish. Place dish in slow cooker; cover and cook on HIGH 2 to 3 hours until edges begin to brown.

4. Remove dish from slow cooker. Cool on wire rack 10 minutes; remove bread from dish and cool completely on wire rack.

Makes 8 to 10 servings

Peach Cobbler

4 large Red Delicious apples

8 tablespoons unsalted butter, melted

⅓ cup chopped macadamia nuts

¼ cup chopped dried apricots

2 tablespoons finely chopped crystallized ginger

1 tablespoon packed dark brown sugar

¾ cup brandy

½ cup vanilla pudding and pie filling mix

2 cups heavy cream

SLOW COOKER DIRECTIONS

1. Slice tops off apples and core; set aside.

2. Combine butter, macadamia nuts, apricots, ginger and brown sugar in medium bowl. Fill cavities of apples with nut mixture. Place apples in slow cooker. Pour brandy into slow cooker. Cover and cook on LOW 4 hours or on HIGH 2 hours.

3. Gently remove apples from slow cooker; set aside and keep warm. Combine pudding mix and cream in small bowl. Add to slow cooker; stir to combine with brandy. Cover and cook on HIGH 30 minutes. Stir until smooth. Serve warm apples with brandy sauce.

Makes 4 servings

Magical Tip

Crystallized (or candied) ginger is fresh ginger that has been cooked in a sugar syrup and then coated with coarse sugar. It is available in some large supermarkets and Asian markets, and can be stored indefinitely in a tightly sealed container. It is most often used as an ingredient in desserts or as a confection.

Baked Ginger Apple

Acknowledgments

**The publisher would like to thank
the companies and organizations listed below
for the use of their recipes in this publication.**

Butterball® Turkey Company

Campbell Soup Company

Perdue Farms Incorporated

Reckitt Benckiser

Unilever Bestfoods North America

Index

Apple
Apple-Date Crisp, 142
Baked Ginger Apples, 154
Butternut Squash-Apple Soup, 28
Campbell's® Golden Mushroom Pork
& Apples, 52
Hot Mulled Cider, 10
Mulled Apple Cider, 16
Red Cabbage and Apples, 134
Spiced Apple & Cranberry Compote,
140
Spiced Apple Tea, 14
Warm Spiced Apples and Pears, 150
Apple-Date Crisp, 142
Asparagus and Cheese Side Dish, 130

Bacon
Festive Bacon & Cheese Dip, 10
Tuscan White Bean Soup, 40
Baked Ginger Apples, 154
Banana-Rum Custard with Vanilla
Wafers, 140
Bananas
Banana-Rum Custard with Vanilla
Wafers, 140
Whole-Grain Banana Bread, 152
Barbara's Pork Chop Dinner, 70
Barbecued Franks, 22
Barbecued Meatballs, 22
Barbecued Pulled Pork, 72
Barbecue Sauce, 78
BBQ Pork Sandwiches, 54
Beans, Canned
Black Bean and Sausage Stew, 72
Chili with Beans & Corn, 26
Easy Vegetarian Vegetable Bean Soup,
30
Moroccan Chicken Tagine, 84
New England Baked Beans, 130
Pesto Rice and Beans, 116
Southwest Bean Chili, 42
Spicy Beans Tex-Mex, 112
Three-bean Turkey Chili, 40
Vegetarian Chili, 38
Beans, Dried
Hearty Lentil Stew, 118
Spicy Beans Tex-Mex, 112
Tuscan White Bean Soup, 40
Beans, Green
Green Bean Casserole, 126
Hearty Lentil Stew, 118
Panama Pork Stew, 80
Pesto Rice and Beans, 116
Stew Provençal, 44

Beef (*see also* **Beef, Ground**)
Beef and Vegetables in Rich
Burgundy Sauce, 68
Beef Stew with Molasses and Raisins,
56
Best Beef Stew, The, 48
Campbell's® Asian Tomato Beef, 50
Campbell's® Savory Pot Roast, 52
Classic Beef & Noodles, 58
Corned Beef and Cabbage, 62
Favorite Beef Stew, 74
Oniony Braised Short Ribs, 67
Steak San Marino, 58
Texas-Style Barbecued Brisket, 78
Beef, Ground
Barbecued Meatballs, 22
Broccoli and Beef Pasta, 64
That's Italian Meat Loaf, 76
Beef and Vegetables in Rich Burgundy
Sauce, 68
Beef Stew with Molasses and Raisins, 56
Best Beef Stew, The, 48
Beverages
Hot Mulled Cider, 10
Mocha Supreme, 12
Mulled Apple Cider, 16
Mulled Wine, 8
Spiced Apple Tea, 14
Triple Delicious Hot Chocolate, 20
Viennese Coffee, 24
Black Bean and Sausage Stew, 72
Breads
Chocolate Chip Lemon Loaf, 148
Honey Whole-Grain Bread, 120
Skinny Cornbread, 126
Spinach Spoonbread, 112
Whole-Grain Banana Bread, 152
Broccoli
Broccoli & Cheese Strata, 116
Broccoli and Beef Pasta, 64
Campbell's® Asian Tomato Beef, 50
Shredded Pork Wraps, 46
Broccoli and Beef Pasta, 64
Broccoli & Cheese Strata, 116
Brunswick Stew, 92
Butternut Squash-Apple Soup, 28

Cabbage
Classic Cabbage Rolls, 54
Corned Beef and Cabbage, 62
Easy Vegetarian Vegetable Bean Soup,
30
Mu Shu Turkey, 98
Red Cabbage and Apples, 134

Cajun Sausage and Rice, 76
Campbell's® Asian Tomato Beef, 50
Campbell's® Creamy Chicken & Wild
Rice, 86
Campbell's® Golden Mushroom Pork &
Apples, 52
Campbell's® Lemon Chicken, 106
Campbell's® Nacho Chicken & Rice
Wraps, 86
Campbell's® Savory Pot Roast, 52
Caponata, 14
Carrots
Beef and Vegetables in Rich
Burgundy Sauce, 68
Beef Stew with Molasses and Raisins,
56
Campbell's® Creamy Chicken &
Wild Rice, 86
Campbell's® Lemon Chicken, 106
Campbell's® Savory Pot Roast, 52
Easy Vegetarian Vegetable Bean Soup,
30
Favorite Beef Stew, 74
Golden Harvest Stew, 62
Hearty Lentil Stew, 118
Hearty Mushroom and Barley Soup,
36
Herbed Chicken & Vegetables, 102
Orange-Spice Glazed Carrots, 128
Steak San Marino, 58
Tuscan White Bean Soup, 40
Cheesy Pork and Potatoes, 60
Cherry
Cherry Rice Pudding, 144
Luscious Pecan Bread Pudding, 146
Cherry Rice Pudding, 144
Chicken
Brunswick Stew, 92
Campbell's® Creamy Chicken &
Wild Rice, 86
Campbell's® Lemon Chicken, 106
Campbell's® Nacho Chicken & Rice
Wraps, 86
Chicken Fajitas with Cowpoke
Barbecue Sauce, 96
Coconut Chicken Curry, 92
Country Captain Chicken, 98
Easy Weeknight Chicken Cacciatore,
108
Forty-Clove Chicken, 88
Harvest Drums, 102
He-Man Stew, 104
Herbed Chicken & Vegetables, 102
Moroccan Chicken Tagine, 84

Chicken (continued)
  90's-Style Slow Cooker Coq au Vin, 90
  Old World Chicken and Vegetables, 100
  Oriental Chicken Wings, 20
  Pineapple Chicken and Sweet Potatoes, 104
  Simple Coq au Vin, 100
  Sweet Chicken Curry, 108
  3-Cheese Chicken & Noodles, 94
Chicken Fajitas with Cowpoke Barbecue Sauce, 96
Chili con Queso, 6
Chilis
  Chili with Beans & Corn, 26
  Southwest Bean Chili, 42
  Three-bean Turkey Chili, 40
  Vegetarian Chili, 38
Chili Turkey Loaf, 90
Chili with Beans & Corn, 26
Chocolate
  Chocolate Chip Lemon Loaf, 148
  Chocolate Croissant Pudding, 136
  Triple Delicious Hot Chocolate, 20
Chocolate Chip Lemon Loaf, 148
Chocolate Croissant Pudding, 136
Classic Beef & Noodles, 58
Classic Cabbage Rolls, 54
Coconut Chicken Curry, 92
Coconut Rice Pudding, 138
Corn
  Chili with Beans & Corn, 26
  Panama Pork Stew, 80
  Potato-Crab Chowder, 36
  Southwest Bean Chili, 42
  Sunshine Squash, 134
  Vegetable-Stuffed Pork Chops, 60
Corned Beef and Cabbage, 62
Country Captain Chicken, 98
Cranberry
  Cran-Orange Acorn Squash, 114
  Curried Snack Mix, 8
  Pumpkin-Cranberry Custard, 146
  Spiced Apple & Cranberry Compote, 140
  Turkey Meatballs in Cranberry-Barbecue Sauce, 18
Cran-Orange Acorn Squash, 114
Curried Snack Mix, 8

Dips
  Chili con Queso, 6
  Easiest Three-Cheese Fondue, 24
  Festive Bacon & Cheese Dip, 10

Easiest Three-Cheese Fondue, 24
Easy Dirty Rice, 114

Easy Vegetarian Vegetable Bean Soup, 30
Easy Weeknight Chicken Cacciatore, 108

Favorite Beef Stew, 74
Festive Bacon & Cheese Dip, 10
Forty-Clove Chicken, 88

Garden Potato Salad, 132
Golden Harvest Stew, 62
Green Bean Casserole, 126

Ham and Potato Casserole, 70
Harvest Drums, 102
Hearty Lentil Stew, 118
Hearty Mushroom and Barley Soup, 36
He-Man Stew, 104
Herbed Chicken & Vegetables, 102
Herbed Turkey Breast with Orange Sauce, 106
Honey Whole-Grain Bread, 120
Hot Mulled Cider, 10

Italian Sausage and Vegetable Stew, 66

Lamb: Classic Cabbage Rolls, 54
Luscious Pecan Bread Pudding, 146

Mediterranean Red Potatoes, 110
Mediterranean Shrimp Soup, 32
Mocha Supreme, 12
Moroccan Chicken Tagine, 84
Mulled Apple Cider, 16
Mulled Wine, 8
Mushrooms
  Beef and Vegetables in Rich Burgundy Sauce, 68
  Easy Weeknight Chicken Cacciatore, 108
  Hearty Mushroom and Barley Soup, 36
  90's-Style Slow Cooker Coq au Vin, 90
  Simple Coq au Vin, 100
  Turkey Mushroom Stew, 82
  Vegetable Pasta Sauce, 122
Mu Shu Turkey, 98

New England Baked Beans, 130
90's-Style Slow Cooker Coq au Vin, 90
Nuts
  Curried Snack Mix, 8
  Luscious Pecan Bread Pudding, 146

Oats
  "Peachy Keen" Dessert Treat, 150
  Apple-Date Crisp, 142

Old World Chicken and Vegetables, 100
Oniony Braised Short Ribs, 67
Orange-Spice Glazed Carrots, 128
Oriental Chicken Wings, 20

Panama Pork Stew, 80
Pasta & Noodles
  Beef and Vegetables in Rich Burgundy Sauce, 68
  Broccoli and Beef Pasta, 64
  Campbell's® Lemon Chicken, 106
  Classic Beef & Noodles, 58
  Harvest Drums, 102
  He-Man Stew, 104
  Old World Chicken and Vegetables, 100
  3-Cheese Chicken & Noodles, 94
Peach Cobbler, 152
"Peachy Keen" Dessert Treat, 150
Pear Crunch, 138
Pears
  Pear Crunch, 138
  Poached Pears with Raspberry Sauce, 144
  Warm Spiced Apples and Pears, 150
Peas: Coconut Chicken Curry, 92
Peppers, Bell
  Barbecued Pulled Pork, 72
  Beef and Vegetables in Rich Burgundy Sauce, 68
  Black Bean and Sausage Stew, 72
  Cajun Sausage and Rice, 76
  Caponata, 14
  Chicken Fajitas with Cowpoke Barbecue Sauce, 96
  Country Captain Chicken, 98
  Easy Dirty Rice, 114
  Garden Potato Salad, 132
  Old World Chicken and Vegetables, 100
  Red Pepper Relish, 12
  Southwest Bean Chili, 42
  Spinach Spoonbread, 112
  Sunshine Squash, 134
  Sweet Chicken Curry, 108
  3-Cheese Chicken & Noodles, 94
  Vegetable Pasta Sauce, 122
  Vegetable-Stuffed Pork Chops, 60
  Vegetarian Chili, 38
Pesto Rice and Beans, 116
Pineapple
  Pear Crunch, 138
  Pineapple Chicken and Sweet Potatoes, 104
Poached Pears with Raspberry Sauce, 144

Pork
Barbara's Pork Chop Dinner, 70
Barbecued Pulled Pork, 72
BBQ Pork Sandwiches, 54
Campbell's® Golden Mushroom Pork & Apples, 52
Cheesy Pork and Potatoes, 60
Golden Harvest Stew, 62
Ham and Potato Casserole, 70
Panama Pork Stew, 80
Pork & Tomato Ragout, 50
Shredded Pork Wraps, 46
Stew Provençal, 44
Sweet and Sour Spare Ribs, 66
That's Italian Meat Loaf, 76
Vegetable-Stuffed Pork Chops, 60
Pork & Tomato Ragout, 50
Potato-Crab Chowder, 36
Potatoes
Barbara's Pork Chop Dinner, 70
Best Beef Stew, The, 48
Brunswick Stew, 92
Campbell's® Savory Pot Roast, 52
Cheesy Pork and Potatoes, 60
Coconut Chicken Curry, 92
Easy Vegetarian Vegetable Bean Soup, 30
Favorite Beef Stew, 74
Garden Potato Salad, 132
Golden Harvest Stew, 62
Ham and Potato Casserole, 70
Herbed Chicken & Vegetables, 102
Mediterranean Red Potatoes, 110
Panama Pork Stew, 80
Pineapple Chicken and Sweet Potatoes, 104
Pork & Tomato Ragout, 50
Potato-Crab Chowder, 36
Rustic Garlic Mashed Potatoes, 118
Scalloped Potatoes and Parsnips, 128
Stew Provençal, 44
Sweet-Spiced Sweet Potatoes, 120
Swiss Cheese Scalloped Potatoes, 124
Puddings & Custards
Banana-Rum Custard with Vanilla Wafers, 140
Cherry Rice Pudding, 144
Chocolate Croissant Pudding, 136
Coconut Rice Pudding, 138
Luscious Pecan Bread Pudding, 146
Pumpkin-Cranberry Custard, 146
Pumpkin-Cranberry Custard, 146

Red Cabbage and Apples, 134
Red Pepper Relish, 12
Rice
Cajun Sausage and Rice, 76
Campbell's® Asian Tomato Beef, 50

Campbell's® Creamy Chicken & Wild Rice, 86
Campbell's® Nacho Chicken & Rice Wraps, 86
Cherry Rice Pudding, 144
Coconut Rice Pudding, 138
Country Captain Chicken, 98
Easy Dirty Rice, 114
Pesto Rice and Beans, 116
Sweet Chicken Curry, 108
Roast Tomato-Basil Soup, 34
Rustic Garlic Mashed Potatoes, 118

Sandwiches & Wraps
Barbecued Pulled Pork, 72
BBQ Pork Sandwiches, 54
Campbell's® Nacho Chicken & Rice Wraps, 86
Chicken Fajitas with Cowpoke Barbecue Sauce, 96
Mu Shu Turkey, 98
Shredded Pork Wraps, 46
Sausage
Barbecued Franks, 22
Best Beef Stew, The, 48
Black Bean and Sausage Stew, 72
Cajun Sausage and Rice, 76
Easy Dirty Rice, 114
Italian Sausage and Vegetable Stew, 66
Scalloped Potatoes and Parsnips, 128
Shellfish
Mediterranean Shrimp Soup, 32
Potato-Crab Chowder, 36
Shredded Pork Wraps, 46
Simple Coq au Vin, 100
Skinny Cornbread, 126
Soups
Butternut Squash-Apple Soup, 28
Easy Vegetarian Vegetable Bean Soup, 30
Hearty Mushroom and Barley Soup, 36
Mediterranean Shrimp Soup, 32
Potato-Crab Chowder, 36
Roast Tomato-Basil Soup, 34
Tuscan White Bean Soup, 40
Southwest Bean Chili, 42
Spiced Apple & Cranberry Compote, 140
Spiced Apple Tea, 14
Spicy Beans Tex-Mex, 112
Spinach Spoonbread, 112
Squash, Summer
Garden Potato Salad, 132
Harvest Drums, 102
Italian Sausage and Vegetable Stew, 66
Vegetable Pasta Sauce, 122

Squash, Winter
Butternut Squash-Apple Soup, 28
Cran-Orange Acorn Squash, 114
Sunshine Squash, 134
Steak San Marino, 58
Stew Provençal, 44
Stews
Beef Stew with Molasses and Raisins, 56
Best Beef Stew, The, 48
Black Bean and Sausage Stew, 72
Brunswick Stew, 92
Favorite Beef Stew, 74
Golden Harvest Stew, 62
Hearty Lentil Stew, 118
He-Man Stew, 104
Italian Sausage and Vegetable Stew, 66
Panama Pork Stew, 80
Pork & Tomato Ragout, 50
Stew Provençal, 44
Turkey Mushroom Stew, 82
Sunshine Squash, 134
Sweet and Sour Spare Ribs, 66
Sweet Chicken Curry, 108
Sweet-Spiced Sweet Potatoes, 120
Swiss Cheese Scalloped Potatoes, 124

Texas-Style Barbecued Brisket, 78
That's Italian Meat Loaf, 76
Three-Bean Turkey Chili, 40
3-Cheese Chicken & Noodles, 94
Tomatoes, Fresh
Chicken Fajitas with Cowpoke Barbecue Sauce, 96
Mediterranean Red Potatoes, 110
Sweet Chicken Curry, 108
Triple Delicious Hot Chocolate, 20
Turkey
Chili Turkey Loaf, 90
Herbed Turkey Breast with Orange Sauce, 106
Mu Shu Turkey, 98
Three-bean Turkey Chili, 40
Turkey Meatballs in Cranberry-Barbecue Sauce, 18
Turkey Mushroom Stew, 82
Turkey Meatballs in Cranberry-Barbecue Sauce, 18
Turkey Mushroom Stew, 82
Tuscan White Bean Soup, 40

Vegetable Pasta Sauce, 122
Vegetable-Stuffed Pork Chops, 60
Vegetarian Chili, 38
Viennese Coffee, 24

Warm Spiced Apples and Pears, 150
Whole-Grain Banana Bread, 152

Index

METRIC CONVERSION CHART

VOLUME MEASUREMENTS (dry)

$\frac{1}{8}$ teaspoon = 0.5 mL
$\frac{1}{4}$ teaspoon = 1 mL
$\frac{1}{2}$ teaspoon = 2 mL
$\frac{3}{4}$ teaspoon = 4 mL
1 teaspoon = 5 mL
1 tablespoon = 15 mL
2 tablespoons = 30 mL
$\frac{1}{4}$ cup = 60 mL
$\frac{1}{3}$ cup = 75 mL
$\frac{1}{2}$ cup = 125 mL
$\frac{2}{3}$ cup = 150 mL
$\frac{3}{4}$ cup = 175 mL
1 cup = 250 mL
2 cups = 1 pint = 500 mL
3 cups = 750 mL
4 cups = 1 quart = 1 L

VOLUME MEASUREMENTS (fluid)

1 fluid ounce (2 tablespoons) = 30 mL
4 fluid ounces ($\frac{1}{2}$ cup) = 125 mL
8 fluid ounces (1 cup) = 250 mL
12 fluid ounces ($1\frac{1}{2}$ cups) = 375 mL
16 fluid ounces (2 cups) = 500 mL

WEIGHTS (mass)

$\frac{1}{2}$ ounce = 15 g
1 ounce = 30 g
3 ounces = 90 g
4 ounces = 120 g
8 ounces = 225 g
10 ounces = 285 g
12 ounces = 360 g
16 ounces = 1 pound = 450 g

DIMENSIONS

$\frac{1}{16}$ inch = 2 mm
$\frac{1}{8}$ inch = 3 mm
$\frac{1}{4}$ inch = 6 mm
$\frac{1}{2}$ inch = 1.5 cm
$\frac{3}{4}$ inch = 2 cm
1 inch = 2.5 cm

OVEN TEMPERATURES

250°F = 120°C
275°F = 140°C
300°F = 150°C
325°F = 160°C
350°F = 180°C
375°F = 190°C
400°F = 200°C
425°F = 220°C
450°F = 230°C

BAKING PAN SIZES

Utensil	Size in Inches/Quarts	Metric Volume	Size in Centimeters
Baking or Cake Pan (square or rectangular)	8×8×2	2 L	20×20×5
	9×9×2	2.5 L	23×23×5
	12×8×2	3 L	30×20×5
	13×9×2	3.5 L	33×23×5
Loaf Pan	8×4×3	1.5 L	20×10×7
	9×5×3	2 L	23×13×7
Round Layer Cake Pan	8×1½	1.2 L	20×4
	9×1½	1.5 L	23×4
Pie Plate	8×1¼	750 mL	20×3
	9×1¼	1 L	23×3
Baking Dish or Casserole	1 quart	1 L	—
	1½ quart	1.5 L	—
	2 quart	2 L	—